ABSTRACT

The study concerns the impact of non-farm employment opportunities on the hired farm labour force and is based on surveys of labour on farms near one new, one expanded and one old-established town in eastern England, supplemented with findings of other British studies on mobility of farm workers. The main questions considered are the influence of distance from urban industrial centres on the rate of labour withdrawal from agriculture, the ways in which occupational mobility occurs and the consequences for workers remaining on farms. Some previous studies have shown that net losses of hired workers are greater from farms near towns, others that urban development helps to stabilise the labour force on nearby farms. In the present study net losses were generally heavier from farms in more isolated areas. The rate at which workers leave farms, their reasons for leaving and subsequent occupations vary with the strength and nature of demand for labour locally and the length of time alternatives have been available. Better terms of employment for farm workers in areas of high labour competition and advantages for their families of proximity to a town also help to retain workers on farms in more urbanised areas.

MOBILITY OF FARM WORKERS

A study of the effects of towns
and industrial employment on
the supply of farm labour

RUTH GASSON

University of Cambridge
Department of Land Economy

Occasional Paper No. 2
1974

Occasional Papers already published in this series:

1. Measurement of Urban Land Use
   R.C.FORDHAM, 1974

2. Mobility of Farm Workers
   RUTH GASSON, 1974

3. Land Reform in Ireland
   T.O'BRIEN and C.F.KOLBERT   (forthcoming)

Obtainable by post, cash with order, from:

   University of Cambridge Department of Land Economy,
   19 Silver Street, Cambridge CB3 9EP.

FOREWORD

by the Professor of Land Economy, University of Cambridge

Land economy is the study of the relationship of human societies to the land, a range and wealth of knowledge covering the ownership, use and development of land in town and country, in regions of industrial and economic development and in the less-developed countries. The subject has many distinct facets of which economic analyses, legal institutions, national and regional planning and the sociology of human habitations and settlements are the main features.

The Department of Land Economy was established in the University of Cambridge in 1961. Its work and influence have grown remarkably since then, at home and overseas, especially when, in 1968, responsibility for agricultural economics was transferred to the Department from the School of Agriculture.

The widened interests and activities of the Department of Land Economy have inspired the publication of this series of occasional papers. While drawing upon the research work of the staff of the Department, the series will include from many quarters of the academic and professional worlds selected texts which relate directly or indirectly to land economy as an academic discipline and research field.

D.R.DENMAN

PREFACE

This report on rural industrialisation and farm labour is a logical development of earlier work by D.M.Turner and D.B.Wallace in the Department of Land Economy, who attempted to measure the volume of employment generated for the indigenous rural population by town expansion schemes under the Town Development Act. Emphasis in the present study is on the way in which industrial development and associated urban growth in rural areas affect farm workers and their families and so determine the supply of labour available for agriculture. This report presents the results of surveys of the changing labour force on farms near new and expanding towns in the eastern region and draws on the findings of other published surveys.

Among the many people who contributed to this study, the author wishes to thank in particular the three hundred farmers in the eastern counties who provided the basic information and Richard Fordham and Mike Turner in the Department of Land Economy for their constructive criticism of earlier drafts of the report.

RUTH GASSON   January 1974.

Ruth Gasson read agriculture at Wye College and studied agricultural economics at Oxford, working in the Agricultural Economics Department at Wye before taking up her present post of Senior Assistant in Research in the Department of Land Economy. Her studies of social change in agriculture have included part time farming in the south east, occupational choice of farmers' sons, mobility of small farmers and, most recently, 'the drift from the land'.

CONTENTS

Part II

1. The farm survey

Since the time of the Black Death, farmers in Britain have been concerned at the continuing decline in the supply of labour available for agriculture. Politicians tend to share their concern, economists to take a more philosophical view. Some whose social consciences are sensitive on this issue would like to see a return to a rural based economy with more labour employed in agriculture. Others feel that farm workers should be allowed a fair share of all the benefits of our predominantly urban civilisation. This study does not set out to attack or to justify 'the drift from the land' nor to predict its effects on farm output. It aims instead to describe some of the factors ·affecting mobility of farm workers with particular emphasis on the influence of towns and alternative employment opportunities. The main questions to be answered are the impact of local employment growth on the farm labour supply, the manner in which occupational mobility comes about and the consequences for workers remaining on farms.

1.1 Scope of the study

This study is based on three surveys of farm labour in the eastern counties, supplemented with data from other sources. The study falls into three parts, the first of which is concerned with changes in the farm labour supply in relation to other employment opportunities. Chapter 1 describes the background to the farm surveys. The second chapter sets the study in its context of a hired farm labour force decreasing in numbers and changing in composition, and indicates some aspects of farm employment in the eastern region and in the survey areas which have a bearing on mobility. Chapter 3 reviews evidence from other studies of the effects of towns and non-farm employment on the supply of farm labour while Chapters 4 and 5 deal with changes in regular and other types of workers in the survey areas in relation to distance from towns. The second part, Chapters 6 and 7, is concerned with workers leaving farms, their reasons for leaving and subsequent occupations. The final part, Chapters 8 and 9, considers workers remaining on farms and the net effects of urban influence and migration of other workers on their conditions of working and living.

1.2 The survey method

Like previous work in this field, the present investigation is a descriptive social survey. The approach has been to describe some of the trends in farm employment and migration in relation to distance from towns and the availability of other jobs, interpreting the survey material in the light of opinions and insights gleaned in the course of the interviews and drawing on the findings of other studies. The survey areas were chosen subjectively to represent the interaction of certain types of urban industrial development with the farm labour force.

The study did not set out to develop and test specific hypotheses about relationships between mobility of farm workers and alternative job opportunities. Such an approach would demand a more rigorous and statistically acceptable method of area sampling. The two approaches should not be mutually exclusive. Rather, the descriptive social survey provides a source from which more precise, quantifiable hypotheses can be drawn and is a necessary precursor to the construction of economic or sociological models.

The rest of this chapter describes the selection of areas and the method of collecting data in the farm surveys. Strength of demand for labour in the three towns and types of farming in the survey areas are described as a background to later chapters.

1.3 Choice of survey areas

1.3.1 *Choice of towns*

Planned development of industry in new and expanded towns will illustrate most clearly the impact of non-farm

2

employment opportunities on the farm labour force. The growth of jobs and population in such towns is rapid and intense, and takes place in areas which were predominantly rural until quite recently. It was argued, therefore, that the effect on the rural labour force should be more apparent than the more gradual development of a longer established urban centre.

Haverhill in West Suffolk, an example of a town expansion scheme, was chosen for the survey together with Stevenage New Town, representing a later stage of urban development, when the town had grown larger and the rural economy had had more time to adjust to the labour demands of the new centre. The planned development of Haverhill and Stevenage, involving transfers of jobs and families from the London area, was concentrated into a short space of time with most new employment being created in manufacturing industry. The city of Cambridge was chosen as a control. Development here has been spread over a much longer period, the range of occupations is wider and the population considerably greater than in Haverhill or Stevenage. Figure 1 shows the location of Haverhill, Stevenage and Cambridge in the eastern region.

1.3.2 Selection of parishes

It was assumed that the towns would exert most influence on employment over a radius of 7 miles. In more sparsely populated areas industrialists may recruit workers from a wider radius (Garbett-Edwards, 1972; Lucey and Kaldor, 1969). Justification for using this cut-off point in the eastern region was provided by a recent survey which showed that only 4 per cent of employees in Haverhill factories lived more than 7 miles from the town (Moseley, 1973). It may be particularly appropriate to study a confined geographical area in the present context, since according to H. Newby, farm workers are obliged to sell their labour in local markets. He considers that while the range of skills possessed by farm workers has become more transferable to other industries and while rural areas have

3.

THE EASTERN REGION

become less isolated from the flow of information about earnings and conditions of employment elsewhere, increasing cost and decreasing frequency of public transport in rural areas may be working against these trends to keep the labour force captive (Newby, 1972a, 1972b).

All parishes lying within or partly within a 7 mile radius of the centre of Haverhill were designated as the survey area. These 58 parishes, covering 120 000 acres of agricultural land, were divided between the counties of Cambridgeshire, Essex and West Suffolk. For Stevenage the survey area was confined to 16 parishes, about 30 000 acres, within the catchment area and lying to the east of the town, in order to avoid overlapping the labour catchment areas of Luton, Hitchin and other nearby towns. It was assumed that for most inhabitants of the survey areas, Haverhill or Stevenage respectively would be the nearest major employment centre. Each survey area was divided into an inner core of parishes within four or five miles of the town and an outer ring, in order to compare the effects of an urban labour market on farms near and farther from the centre.

In the case of Cambridge, parishes were sampled over a wider radius in order to investigate the labour situation on farms beyond the conventional boundaries of the labour catchment area. Three groups of parishes were chosen. The nearer group consisted of Cambridge itself and four adjacent parishes, the middle area two contiguous parishes about ten miles from the city and the farthest, one large parish some twenty miles by road from Cambridge. These parishes together accounted for 31 000 acres of farm land.

1.4 The farm surveys

In order to give a final sample of about 100 farms in each area, all holdings above 100 standard man days in a representative sample of Haverhill parishes and in all but three of the Stevenage parishes were contacted. As the smaller holdings were found to employ very few hired workers, only holdings above 600 standard man days in the Cambridge survey area were included. The final sample consisted of 96 Haverhill, 98 Stevenage and 98 Cambridge farms out of 100, 106 and 101 originally contacted. The remaining farmers were not operating genuine agricultural business or were otherwise unwilling or unable to co-operate. Haverhill farmers were interviewed during May 1970, the Stevenage farmers between June and September 1971 and the Cambridge sample from March to May 1972. Information was collected on the current labour force including farmers and family workers, their ages, lengths of service and conditions of employment, numbers of workers employed on the holding five and ten years previously and on all workers leaving farms over this period, their subsequent occupations and reasons for leaving.

1.5 Employment in the survey towns

1.5.1 *Haverhill Town Expansion Scheme*
Haverhill was traditionally a centre for the manufacture of textiles and clothing, heavily dependent on a single firm which reached its peak in about 1900. According to T. Eastwood, the subsequent decline of Haverhill was partly due to economic stagnation in the textile industry but in addition, Haverhill was unusually dependent on female labour. Imbalance of employment between the sexes is a potent cause of out-migration and between the two world wars the population decreased by a quarter. Eastwood considered manufacturing industry in Haverhill would probably cease to grow without an external stimulus in view of the population decline, imbalance of male and female employment, low standards of local services and poor accessibility to larger industrial centres in the region (Eastwood, 1951).

The necessary stimulus was given by the Town Development Act, under which Haverhill became an expanded town, receiving the first families in 1959. Between 1961 and 1971 the population more than doubled and the target has since been

6

raised to 30 000. Most newcomers are from London but families have migrated to Haverhill from other parts of West Suffolk and elsewhere in East Anglia, despite the deterrent effect of new housing being reserved primarily for London overspill (West Suffolk County Planning Department, 1968). Employment is largely in manufacturing industry, including timber and furniture, clothing and plastics, but there are also firms concerned with engineering and food processing in the district.

1.5.2 *Stevenage New Town*

Old Stevenage, situated on the Great North Road thirty miles north of London, owed much of its early development to coach traffic. With the decline of coaching in the nineteenth century and the loss of its agricultural market the importance of Stevenage diminished. In an area of small country towns it never became a dominant centre, being overshadowed by the growing industrial complex of Luton and Dunstable to the west and competing with Letchworth, Hitchin and Baldock to the north and Welwyn Garden City to the south. It exercised most attraction for rural parishes to the east but even here the rural population was declining.

In 1946 Stevenage was designated as the site for a new town to help relieve congestion and ease the housing shortage in London. When development began in 1949 the population was about 6 000. By 1971 it had risen to 67 000 and the target is now 150 000. As with Haverhill, most employment in the new town is in manufacturing with computers, aircraft and photographic processing among the firms represented.

1.5.3 *Cambridge as an employment centre*

With a population of 100 000, Cambridge is considerably larger than the other towns. It serves as an administrative centre for the region as well as being a university town and so offers more employment in white collar and service occupations. There is, nevertheless, a substantial amount of industry in the city and surrounding villages, including electronics, engineering and food processing, and the manufacture of fertilisers, cement, paper, and glue.

1.5.4 Town expansion and employment of the local population

Although the primary aims of planned decentralisation of industry are to relieve congestion in the conurbations and provide jobs and homes for the homeless, the indigenous population is necessarily drawn into the schemes. D. M. Turner (1966) measured the employment generated for local people by the expansion of Thetford in Norfolk and Haverhill, from the inception of the development schemes in 1959. He found that while the London overspill population benefitted first from the creation of new jobs, within a few years Londoners and locals were filling new vacancies in equal numbers. Of particular relevance to the present study was the finding that over time, the recruitment of workers from villages and rural areas surrounding the towns increased markedly. If this trend continued, it would be reasonable to assume that growing numbers of rural and farm workers would be drawn to work in the expanding towns from an ever-widening radius.

A later study of Haverhill and Thetford by M.J. Moseley (1973) suggests that the relationship between industrial growth and recruitment of rural workers is not so straightforward. During the early years of development, employers recruit labour mainly within the expanding town and as this labour supply is taken up there comes a rapid increase in recruitment from surrounding rural areas. Whether, after this initial phase, industrial firms recruit more workers from within the urban areas or from surrounding villages will depend on the rate of growth in demand for labour and the possibility of satisfying this demand *in situ*. If demand is strong, it is likely that substantial numbers of workers will be drawn in from rural areas and from farms. If demand is weaker, recruitment may be largely confined to the town (Moseley, 1973).

8

Most industrialists approached in the *Small Towns Study* agreed that they recruited workers mainly from agriculture but in Wisbech where unemployment was highest, other manufacturing firms were considered to be the main source of recruits (East Anglia Consultative Committee, 1972). This supports Moseley's hypothesis.

1.5.5 *Strength of demand for labour in the survey towns*

Moseley suggested that the rate of recruitment of rural workers to jobs in the towns would depend on the length of time the urban labour market had been operating and the buoyancy of demand for labour. A case could be made for each of the towns having a greater impact on farm workers than the other two. Haverhill's development was the most recent and for this reason it might be expected to have had greatest influence on employment patterns during the 1960s. Cambridge, having been established as an employment centre for longest, should by this token have had the least effect on the rural labour force.

Demand for labour must be related to the size of the urban labour force and the absolute number of job vacancies. In June 1969, 7 800 persons were registered in employment in Haverhill Employment Exchange area, 31 700 in Stevenage and 76 700 in Cambridge. On this basis the attraction of Cambridge should be greatest, Haverhill least. (These figures exaggerate the number of jobs in Cambridge itself since the Employment Exchange area includes a number of rural parishes).

Recruitment depends also on the rate of growth in employment according to Moseley. On this score Stevenage should be the strongest magnet, Cambridge the weakest. Between 1960 and 1969 total employment increased by 53 per cent in Stevenage, 37 per cent in Haverhill and 27 per cent in Cambridge. The level of unemployment is another measure of the strength of demand for labour. As Appendix Table A1.1 shows, rates of unemployment during the 1960s were always higher in Haverhill than the other towns, rarely exceeding one per cent in the Stevenage area. Despite the fact that Stevenage

9

may have been growing faster in its initial phase in the 1950s, it achieved higher rates of growth than Haverhill or Cambridge throughout the 1960s.

In short, the significance of the Haverhill expansion scheme is that it occured the most recently; its first impact would have been experienced during the ten year period covered by the farm survey. The opportunity for non-farm employment in the Cambridge and Stevenage areas was of less recent origin but here the demand for labour was more insistent. Good communications with London, the Midlands and North have contributed to the economic success of Stevenage and to a smaller extent, of Cambridge. The slower growth of Haverhill may be partly attributable to its location. Although only about sixty miles from London, its communications with the city and other regions of the country are far from ideal, nor is it easily accessible to the east coast ports or to other industrial centres in East Anglia. Timing of development may also have an effect on the potential for growth. Stevenage started to expand at a time of full employment whereas Haverhill was launched during a period of slower growth in the national economy.

1.6   Types of farming

The type of farming will influence the size of the labour force and the types of workers required. In most respects the pattern of farming found near Cambridge is similar to that throughout the Haverhill and Stevenage areas but unlike that in the Fens.

The Stevenage and Haverhill areas are superficially alike with undulating topography and soils derived mainly from chalk and boulder clay. Land in the Stevenage area is mostly between 300 and 500 feet, in Haverhill between 200 and 400 feet. With the exception of the city itself, most land in the Cambridge survey area is in the Black Fens, all below 200 feet and predominantly flat with soils derived from fen peat and underlying clay. Types of farming in the three areas are broadly similar with heavy emphasis on arable crops, particularly cereals and cash roots, and with few livestock. More than 80 per cent of the output from Haverhill and Cambridge farms comes from crops with wheat, barley, potatoes and sugar beet contributing more than half. Livestock are more important in the Stevenage area, where beef and dairy cattle account for almost one quarter of total output but even here, crops still provide the greater part. Horticulture is insignificant in the Haverhill and Stevenage areas but accounts for almost one third of the output of Cambridge farms, mainly as top fruit and vegetables grown on a field scale.

Intensity of land use on Cambridge farms, measured in terms of standard man days per acre, is much higher than in the other areas. Consequently size of holdings tends to be smaller, averaging only 68 acres in the Cambridge area compared with 206 acres for Stevenage and 233 acres for Haverhill farms. Size distribution of holdings is very similar for the Haverhill and Stevenage areas, but the Cambridge area has more small holdings.

Livestock production is more important near each of the towns. Otherwise there is no distinct pattern of change in type of farming, land use or farm size according to distance from towns. Horticultural crops, for instance, are more important for farms closer to Stevenage and Cambridge than farther away but more important for farms distant from Haverhill than for those near the town.

2. Mobility of the farm labour force

Following the general description of the survey areas in Chapter 1, this chapter discusses farm employment in these areas, in the eastern region and in the country as a whole and indicates some of the features which affect labour mobility.

2.1 Mobility of farmers and farm workers

It is hired workers rather than farmers or members of their families who are leading the exodus (Hirsch, 1951 and 1955; Bellerby, 1958; Thomas, 1965; Heath and Whitby, 1969). Between 1851 and 1951 the number of hired workers on farms in England and Wales fell from 1 268 000 to 483 000, a decrease of 62 per cent, numbers of relatives assisting on farms fell from 112 000 to 88 000 (21 per cent), while numbers of farmers rose slightly, from 249 000 to 263 000 over the century. M. C. Whitby (1966) showed that numbers of farmers decreased after 1951. Even so, the hired workers' contribution to the labour force has continued to decrease and the farmers' share has increased from about one sixth in 1851 to over one third today. In June 1972 the regular labour force on farms in England and Wales consisted of 226 000 farmers, partners and directors of farming companies, 74 000 family workers and 204 000 hired non-family workers. Farmers and other family workers thus outnumbered regular hired workers by three to two.

Similar trends have been observed in other countries. In the Republic of Ireland (Walsh, 1971) and in the Federal German Republic (Priebe, 1969) for example, the hired component of the agricultural labour force declined sharply between 1950 and the late 1960s. Analysis of a one per cent sample of the labour force in the United States for the years 1957 to 1963 showed that off-farm mobility rates were always higher for hired workers than for farmers (Hathaway and Perkins, 1968).

There are many economic, social and psychological reasons why hired workers should be more inclined than farmers to leave agriculture. Farmers usually have more to lose and less to gain, both financially and in terms of social status, through giving up farming (Bellerby, 1956; Nalson, 1968; Gasson, 1969b, 1973). Workers have less opportunity to exercise control over processes and events in the course of their work than their employers and may therefore derive less satisfaction from the job. D. Hodson (1969) suggests that workers may be more restricted than farmers in their social circle and leisure activities and so stand to gain less satisfaction outside working hours.

Farm family workers are usually less mobile than other hired workers as a result of socialisation in the farm family and in the expectation of inheriting the farm business (Gasson, 1968, 1969a.) Current income and working conditions for them may be no better, often rather worse, than for other hired workers but their future prospects are usually brighter. If one member of the labour force has to be made redundant, for example, it is not usually the farmer's son who is dismissed. With many hired workers leaving the land, too, farmers may take their sons into partnership rather earlier than they would otherwise have done, so offering them a greater incentive to remain in farming.

The study will concentrate on mobility of hired farm workers because they contribute most to 'the drift from the land.' The next section describes the size and composition of the farm labour force in the eastern region[1] and in the survey areas and the following section discusses features of the farm labour force which have particular significance for mobility.

2.2 Agricultural labour in the region and in the survey areas

Agriculture is more important in the economy of the eastern region than in the country as a whole. In 1966 the region had

1 The eastern region as defined by the Ministry of Agriculture, Fisheries and Food at the time of the survey comprised the counties of Bedfordshire, Cambridgeshire, the Isle of Ely, Essex, Hertfordshire, Huntingdonshire and the Soke of Peterborough, the Holland division of Lincolnshire, Norfolk and Suffolk.

13

8.4 per cent of the nation's occupied population but 16.1 per cent of those occupied in agriculture. Farms tend to be larger and to employ more labour than in other parts of the country. In June 1972, 52 000 of the 204 000 regular farm workers and farm managers in England and Wales were in this region while farmers and family workers were less well represented (Table 2.1).

Table 2.1   The eastern region's contribution to the national farm labour force 1972

	England and Wales	Eastern region	Per cent in region
	000s	000s	
Farmers, partners and directors	226.0	32.1	14.2
Regular family workers	73.9	10.2	13.8
Farm managers and regular hired workers	204.1	51.8	25.4
Seasonal and casual workers	67.1	14.7	21.9
Total agricultural labour force*	571.0	108.8	19.0

Source: Ministry of Agriculture, Fisheries and Food, June census 1972.

*Components do not always add up to totals due to rounding.

The composition of the hired labour force is similar to that for the country as a whole except that full time adult male and female workers are rather more important here, youths considerably less so (Appendix Table A2.1). The small number of boys employed on farms in eastern arable and market gardening areas in contrast with the large numbers in the uplands of the north and west was remarked upon by J. Carter and G. P. Hirsch (1952). Seasonal labour appears to be rather more important in the eastern counties than elsewhere; of the

67 000 seasonal and casual workers on farms on the day of the 1972 June census, 15 000 were in the eastern region. As in the rest of the country, the hired farm labour force in the eastern region is predominantly male with most workers employed full time, that is working for forty hours or more each week throughout the year. About half the part time and more than half the seasonal workers are female.

The composition of the hired farm labour force in the Stevenage and Haverhill areas is similar to that near Cambridge (Appendix Table A2.2) with rather more full time and fewer seasonal and female workers than the region as a whole. Farms in the more rural parishes employ relatively more full time regular workers and consequently have a higher proportion of men in the labour force. Greater reliance on part time and seasonal labour near the towns is associated with greater employment of females. Garden centres and small market gardens, often situated on the outskirts of a town, employ women on a seasonal basis while plant nurseries may employ women as florists on a regular basis throughout the year. For the rest of the Cambridge survey area the use of labour reflects the distinctive pattern of Fen farming. At the time of the June agricultural census these farms would employ large numbers of seasonal and casual workers for hoeing and singling sugar beet and hence the farm labour force includes many more women and fewer full time male workers than the other areas.

2.3 Factors affecting mobility of farm workers

Certain characteristics of the labour force in the eastern region suggest that mobility might be greater here than elsewhere. Hired workers accounted for 55 per cent of the regular farm labour force in the region compared with 41 per cent nationally. A high ratio of hired workers to farmers and family members implies high mobility rates, for the reasons discussed in section 2.1 above. The predominance of large, arable farms may also be conducive to mobility. Mechanisation has allowed more labour to be released from arable farms than from livestock farms in recent decades. Workers on large farms are more likely than those on smaller farms to change jobs. The survey of the agricultural labour force in England and Wales carried out by the National Economic Development Office in 1970 showed that 55 per cent of hired workers on farms below 100 acres had remained on the same farm since entering agricultural employment compared with only 34 per cent on farms of 500 acres and over (Agriculture E.D.C., 1972). Small farms rely more on family workers, who would be less likely to move, and on youths who have had less time in which to do so. The potential for mobility may therefore be higher in the eastern region than in northern and western Britain where farms tend to be smaller, concentrating on livestock production and relying heavily on family labour.

While the structure of the farm labour force in the eastern region may favour mobility, characteristics of workers themselves are less likely to be associated with high rates of occupational mobility and migration. Mobility is influenced by age, sex, marital status and family ties, education, qualifications and training and by present employment status.

Mobility tends to decrease with age since older workers normally find it harder to adapt to new tasks and new work situations and employers are usually less anxious to train men for new jobs after about the middle forties. The average age of hired farm workers in the East Anglia Economic Planning Region, 42.3 years, is substantially above the national average of 35.5 years (Agriculture E.D.C., 1972). Farms in the eastern region have a preponderence of older workers and as Table 2.2 shows, more than 40 per cent of hired workers in the region are within 30 years of retirement compared with less than one third nationally. Although mobility among the existing labour force may not, for this reason, be as serious in the region as in other parts of the country, the question of replacement is more imminent here than elsewhere.

In the survey area generally, fewer young men, more over 45s, are to be found on farms near the towns compared with

16

the more rural areas. In the Haverhill survey area, however, the position is reversed with a rather younger labour force employed on farms near the town (Appendix Table A2.3).

Table 2.2 Age distribution of full time hired male workers in England and Wales and the eastern region, 1969.

	England and Wales	Eastern region
	pe per cent	pe per cent
Under 18	7.3	4.5
18–19	5.9	3.9
20–24	13.6	9.7
25–34	20.5	17.8
35–44	20.2	22.1
45–64	29.8	38.8
65 and over	2.7	3.2
All male workers	100.0	100.0
Numbers	231 000	53 838

Source: Ministry of Agriculture, Fisheries and Food, June census 1969.

Wastage of young workers has long been recognised as a problem for the industry (e.g. Britton and Smith, 1947; Hughes, 1957; Thomas, 1965; Whitby, 1967; Bessell, 1972). Although farms in the eastern counties employ relatively few youths they continue to suffer heavy losses. Hirsch (1955) noted earlier that regular workers have been leaving agriculture more rapidly than temporary workers, males more rapidly than females and youths more rapidly than adults. While these trends were fairly consistent for the eastern region and for the country as a whole during the 1960s, Appendix Table A2.4 shows that losses from the region of youths employed full time, part time and seasonally all exceeded the national rates of loss. Workers aged 25 and under in the N.E.D.O. survey were asked if they expected to be working on the land in five years' time; 26.4 per cent of young workers on East Anglian farms thought they would not, as compared with 17.0 per cent for England and Wales as a whole (Bessell, 1972).

Education and vocational training enhance mobility, another reason for limited mobility among farm workers in the eastern region. The N.E.D.O. survey showed that East Anglian farm workers had left school rather earlier than the average for all farm workers and that fewer had any educational or agricultural qualifications or had had any formal training in agriculture (Table 2.3). This would be due in part to their high average age since young workers are considerably more likely than older men to have stayed on at school, gained educational certificates and received some formal education and training in agriculture. Lack of other work experience may also restrict mobility, limiting the choice of jobs to those requiring a minimum of previously acquired skill and training. According to the N.E.D.O. survey 83 per cent of farm workers in East Anglia, compared with 80 per cent nationally had never worked anywhere but on the land.

Table 2.3   Education and training of farm workers in England and Wales and in East Anglia, 1970.

	England and Wales	East Anglia
Mean age leaving school (years)	14.7	14.4
	per cent of workers	
Educational qualification	9.9	5.6
Agricultural qualification	9.5	7.2
Agricultural training	12.6	8.8
Training on family farm	26.8	18.2

Source: Agriculture EDC, 1972, *Agricultural Manpower in England and Wales*

The Wages and Employment Enquiry carried out annually by the Ministry of Agriculture on a sample of some 4 000 holdings in England and Wales shows that dairy cowmen and other stockmen tend to be the most mobile within agriculture, staying for the shortest time on one farm. Foremen and bailiffs, tractor drivers and general farm workers remain in their jobs for longest and these categories would include the majority of farm workers in the eastern region. Where livestock enterprises are more important, that is nearer each of the towns in the survey and especially in the Stevenage area, farmers may encounter greater problems in recruiting, replacing and housing their stockmen.

As Appendix Table A2.4 shows, seasonal and casual workers have not been leaving the land as rapidly as regular workers in recent years. Seasonal and casual workers include many housewives, students, school children, pensioners and men with other part time occupations who are not in a position to take full time employment outside agriculture or who may be restricted in their choice of jobs by lack of transport. Greater use of seasonal and casual labour near the towns of Haverhill and Stevenage might therefore be expected to limit mobility here compared with farms in the remoter parishes. Where large numbers of seasonal workers are employed, as in the Fens, the workers are likely to be well organised and rates for the job are negotiated through a gangmaster rather than on an individual basis. This might mean that the seasonal workers employed near the towns would react in a different way to changing job opportunities from the members of seasonal labour gangs in the Fens.

While the high ratio of hired workers to farm family members and the predominance of large, arable farms in the eastern region and the survey areas might be expected to result in a rapid outflow of labour, the high average age of workers in the region, their low levels of educational and vocational qualifications and their farm employment status all suggest low rates of mobility. Although farms in this region employ relatively few youths, the probability of these young workers making lifelong careers in agriculture is fairly low. The net effect for the region of these opposing influences in recent years has been for the farm labour force to decline as rapidly as in the

19

rest of the country but with a faster outflow of youths and a correspondingly slower reduction among other categories of workers. This chapter has considered factors within the labour force which influence labour mobility. The following chapter discusses the evidence that external forces affect mobility from agriculture.

3. Access to towns and to other jobs

This chapter reviews evidence from other studies of relationships between access to towns, opportunities for non-farm employment and the supply of labour available for agriculture. Through improved access to centres of employment and creation of new jobs in rural areas, more opportunities are becoming available to the rural population. The building of a motorway or a power station in a rural area may generate a large amount of employment during the construction phase without causing any permanent increase in employment locally. Rural industrialisation more often involves the establishment of factories in small country towns, resulting in permanent increases in local population and employment. The supply of labour available for agriculture is affected in two ways. First, some farm workers will be attracted to jobs in new industries or in service occupations which expand to meet the needs of the growing population. Second, improvements in the range and quality of urban amenities and services, stimulated by the growth of population and economic activity, can be enjoyed by the indigenous rural population, thus affecting the lives of those who remain on farms. Changes in the supply of labour available for agriculture and growth of an urban population have further implications for farm structure, production and labour use. Each aspect will be discussed in turn, making reference to some of the relevant published studies.

3.1 Losses of workers to other industries

The *Report of the Committee on Land Utilisation in Rural Areas* (Scott Report) published in 1942 reflects a wide range of attitudes towards provision of alternative employment in the countryside. The majority of the Scott Committee feared that large scale industrial development might harm agriculture by attracting labour, especially younger workers, away from the land and that rural communities might be adversely affected as a result of conflict between rural and urban mentalities. Their objection to factories being sited in agricultural communities was partly based on the fear that this would attract labour from the land and so prejudice the expansion of food production, then so vital to national survival.

Provision of alternative employment has usually, but not always, been shown to result in a more rapid reduction in the local farm labour force. Evidence to the House of Commons Select Committee on Agriculture suggested that farmers located near large towns or close to industry were experiencing more difficulty in obtaining labour than those in rural areas and that proximity to building sites or construction of roads or power stations posed problems for some. Analysis of outflows of labour from agriculture between 1964 and 1965 in selected counties showed that highest losses had occured near conurbations (Ministry of Agriculture, Fisheries and Food, 1968). Comparisons of parish statistics for 1941 and 1964 for parts of Kent and East Sussex showed that the rate of reduction in employment of farm labour decreased with increasing distance from London (Gasson, 1966, 57—60). Mobility of young hired workers from Irish farms was found to be positively associated with availability of non-farm jobs (Walsh 1971). In the Vale of Evesham in the early 1960s advent of industry was causing an acute shortage of labour for agriculture (Woods, 1968). Evidence to the Commission on the Third London Airport, presented on behalf of the Nuthampstead Preservation Society, suggested that if the airport were to be located there, provision of employment in offices and factories in the vicinity would attract workers from agriculture, reducing productivity on farms or pushing up operating costs substantially (Nardecchia, 1969). More recently the high wages offered by North Sea oil companies have resulted in unprecedented outflows of farm workers from Easter Ross, the Black Isle and parts of Inverness-shire and further developments are expected to attract workers from Aberdeenshire farms (Farmers Weekly 1973a).

Other evidence is equivocal or even contradictory. Analysis of labour losses by county for England and Wales for the years 1949 to 1965 showed that losses of regular whole time workers were heaviest in Anglesey, Caernarvon, Glamorgan, Merioneth and Rutland, of which only Glamorgan could be regarded as an industrialised county at that time. Greatest reductions in part time, seasonal and casual labour occurred in three counties with a substantial industrial base (Cheshire, Leicestershire and Warwickshire) and five predominantly rural (Caernarvonshire, Cornwall, Denbighshire, the Isle of Wight and Rutland) (Ministry of Agriculture, Fisheries and Food, 1967, 16—18). In the United States, too, off-farm mobility is not a simple function of distance from major labour markets. Although mobility rates for the nation as a whole were highest for people living within fifty miles of a city, the pattern varied between regions and was sometimes reversed (Hathaway and Perkins, 1968).

Some studies have found heaviest rates of outflow from farms which are less accessible to towns or other employment centres. In some cases there has even been an increase in employment on farms near towns. Labour losses from farms in the Cambridge sub-region illustrate this tendency. The sub-region includes Cambridgeshire and parts of Bedfordshire, Essex, Hertfordshire, Huntingdonshire, the Isle of Ely and West Suffolk. It encompasses the city of Cambridge and the smaller towns of Biggleswade, Ely, Haverhill, Huntingdon, Newmarket, Royston, Saffron Walden and St Neots. The 292 parishes in the sub-region were divided into 'accessible' and 'remote' on the basis of linear distance and frequency of bus service to their nearest town. Remote parishes as a whole lost 37.5 per cent of their hired farm workers in the period 1961 to 1969, accessible parishes only 27.3 per cent (Appendix Table A3.1). Only two of the seven districts individually did not follow this pattern. It was consistent for almost all categories of workers (adult men, youths and females employed full time, part time or temporarily). Particularly striking was the fact that employment

23

of women and girls on farms in 'remote' parishes decreased by 39.4 per cent, but in accessible parishes by only 3.2 per cent.

While some studies have shown that proximity to non-farm employment causes heavier migration from agriculture, others suggest that workers are encouraged to remain on farms near towns while leaving more remote areas. The apparent contradiction may reflect the varying lengths of time for which the rural population has been exposed to other job opportunities. As C. E. Bishop has pointed out, while the exodus from agriculture in advanced industrial countries has been particularly heavy near centres of industrial growth, 'The pattern of migration of people from farms within countries varies with the stage of economic development. An expansion of non-agricultural employment initially draws labour from the farms in contiguous areas. Since the pattern of industrial development has been quite variable within most countries, this has meant that population pressure tended to accumulate in remote rural areas. In most countries ... industrial development has become so extensive and dispersed that the highest rates of migration from agriculture are now occurring in the remote agricultural areas' (Bishop, 1965, 30).

It could be added that when the farm labour force has been exposed to alternative employment opportunities for some time, potentially mobile workers will already have left and those remaining on farms will be largely the ones who are less willing or less able to leave. Alternative employment will have to be made more attractive to draw out the remaining workers. At the same time, farmers who have lost some workers to other employment may be stimulated to improve conditions of employment for those they wish to retain.

3.2 Improvements in rural standards of living

The length of time a rural population has been exposed to other opportunities could help to account for varying rates of migration from agriculture. If the labour force has been stabilised on farms near towns, it may be because access to towns with their varying services and facilities is regarded favourably by farm workers and their families. The majority of the Scott Committee agreed there would be certain advantages in establishing industry in the countryside. Factories would bring in their wake improvements in electricity, gas and water supplies, education and vocational training facilities, helping to raise standards of living in rural areas. Suitable industries, meaning those closely connected with agriculture or relying heavily on female or juvenile labour, might provide employment for farm workers in winter and for rural workers' wives, and encourage more young people to remain in the rural area.

One member of the Scott Committee, S. R. Dennison, presented a minority report in which he made a strong case for creating new employment in the countryside in order to absorb those displaced from farms, provide opportunities for members of their families and offer a wider choice of jobs to young people. He argued that introduction of industry offered the best prospect of improving social and economic conditions in the countryside and suggested that the most difficult cases would not be those rural areas where new developments were likely to occur but those where employment and economic development remained static. Later J. Saville, writing on rural depopulation in England and Wales, concluded that 'integration of new industrial devlopment in the countryside would make immeasurably better conditions of living and working there and would permit a rebuilding and revitalising of lively social units in rural areas.' (Saville, 1957, 171).

Evidence from a number of studies supports this view. Development of Scunthorpe in Lincolnshire as an industrial centre with its shopping, entertainment and other services was judged to have been responsible for stabilising the farming element in accessible villages at a time of general exodus from rural parts of the county (Agricultural Land Service, 1951). Although most of the evidence to the Select Committee on

Agriculture suggested labour shortages were more acute on farms near large towns, there were reports of farmers in isolated areas like the Pennines and the Lincolnshire Wolds having difficulty in keeping workers because wives disliked the remoteness, poor housing and general lack of amenities (Ministry of Agriculture, Fisheries and Food, 1968). W. R. Hall predicted that farmers on the rural urban fringe would have most difficulty in keeping labour because of proximity to urban employment and because farm workers would mix frequently with urban workers. He found, however, that recruitment was not a problem for farmers on the outskirts of the Birmingham conurbation, several suggesting that they enjoyed an advantage over farmers in more rural areas since proximity to urban facilities was an attraction to workers and their wives (Hall, 1970). Only 12 per cent of farmers in the area of Buckinghamshire designated for the new city of Milton Keynes felt they had experienced greater difficulty in recruiting labour as a result of urban development (Reading University, 1971).

In a very different setting, a study of the socio-economic situation of workers on state farms in regions of Poland undergoing rapid industrialisation revealed that, contrary to expectation, inflows of workers exceeded outflows on farms near the industrial centres. This was attributed to more favourable conditions of employment on farms near town and benefits from access to the towns, including better shops, improved commercial and medical services, easier communications, more cultural contacts and better opportunities for education and vocational training for the young. In addition, sons and daughters might work off the state farm and so supplement family income considerably (Ignar, 1971).

3.3 Effects on agricultural production

Whether 'the drift from the land' has been accelerated or reduced by the growth of non-farm employment, there is little evidence that farm production has suffered. The fears of the majority of the Scott Committee seem now to have been groundless in that a rapid outflow of hired labour from farms since the war has not prevented output from rising. Whether output would have increased more if workers had not left, and for how long the industry should allow the labour force to shrink at its present rate, are difficult to determine. As A. P. Power and S. A. Harris have pointed out, there is an important distinction to be made between a reduction in the size of the agricultural labour force and an agricultural industry suffering from a labour shortage. The notion of a labour shortage is only meaningful in relation to a specified production target which has not been achieved (Power and Harris, 1973).

Expansion of non-farm employment undoubtedly causes severe labour problems for some farms . Yet there are many examples of proximity to an urban labour market stimulating an increase in forms of production like horticulture, which are more labour intensive. Although the 'pull' of other employment opportunities may be strong the 'push' from agriculture is reduced. H. E. Bracey found, for example, that development of the Fawley oil refinery in Hampshire had apparently led to an increase in employment on farms in the district, because the land was being farmed more intensively (Bracey, 1963). In Brabant in the Netherlands it was observed that peasant farms near industrial centres were turning to horticultural production to supply fresh fruit and vegetables demanded by the growing industrial population (Kotter, 1962).

In the Cambridge sub-region, labour requirements for farming had increased by 12.0 per cent in accessible parishes as a whole between 1961 and 1969 but decreased by 4.0 per cent for all remote parishes. In all but one of the individual districts, labour requirements had increased near the town relative to more rural parishes. Every major farm enterprise but poultry showed the same tendency to increase more or decrease less nearer towns. For horticulture this was particularly marked, labour requirements increasing by one third in accessible parishes but only by one fortieth in remote parishes. (Here the growing industrial population was perhaps less interested in

27

supplies of fresh fruit and vegetables than in flowers, plants and garden services.) This helps to account for the smaller reduction in employment on farms near towns than in more rural areas. Clearly, proximity to the towns had not prevented farmers from embarking on labour intensive enterprises.

Provision of alternative employment in rural areas may prove beneficial to farming because it allows the potential labour surplus to be removed rather sooner than otherwise. This can have favourable effects on farm structure and production. The net effect of large scale construction schemes on farming in north Wales, for instance, was to speed up mechanisation on farms which were previously overstaffed, with a consequent improvement in farm incomes and little if any reduction in output (Jones, 1972). One surprising result of locating industrial plants in remote areas of western Ireland was to increase output on farms whose occupiers had gone to work in the factories (Lucey and Kaldor, 1969). In West Germany the net result of rural industrialisation has been improved agrarian structure, greater labour productivity and better living and working conditions for those remaining on farms (International Labour Office, 1960, 64–66).

To summarise, although provision of non-farm employment in rural areas has usually been shown to cause a more rapid outflow of labour from farms, some studies show no direct relationship between mobility rates and distance from industrial centres, and some even suggest a reversal of the expected trend. These discrepancies might reflect the differing lengths of time for which other work has been available to the farm labour force. Where the farm labour force has been stabilised near towns, advantages of urban proximity may have outweighed the attractions of non-farm employment for the remaining farm workers. Little evidence can be found to show that growth of non-farm employment has had an adverse effect on farm output; in some instances the growing urban population has stimulated more intensive forms of production. Provision of alternative employment may in fact assist restructuring of farm units or encourage investment.

4. Changes in farm labour in the survey areas

The first question to be answered was how the presence of an urban labour market affects the rate of outflow of workers from nearby farms. Some of the studies reviewed in Chapter 3 showed that net losses of hired workers had been greater near towns and industrial centres, others that development of towns had helped to stabilise the labour force on surrounding farms. The composition of the labour force on farms in the survey areas gave equally confusing impressions. Housewives, part time workers and older men, who were more numerous on farms near the towns, are less liable to change jobs than youths and younger men, who contributed more to the labour force in wholly rural areas, but on the other hand, farms nearer the towns employed more stockmen and stockmen are more mobile than arable workers.

The answer to this question was equivocal. It was found that while turnover of labour was generally higher near the towns, net losses of workers were *greater* from farms near Haverhill but *smaller* from farms near Stevenage and Cambridge than from the surrounding rural areas. This conclusion was based on two sources of information. Parish summaries of the June returns for 1960 and 1969 gave complete coverage of all agricultural holdings in the survey areas but did not cover farmers or family workers. The farm survey provided a comparison over ten years of the use of regular labour, including farm family members, for the farms visited but since information was collected retrospectively from occupiers of farms which had been in operation in 1970–2, those which had changed hands within the decade or ceased to operate as separate units could not be included in the analysis. Existing farms had generally increased their acreage or otherwise expanded the scale of operations over the survey period so comparisons of labour use over time will underestimate the full extent of labour saving achieved. Only larger farms were visited in the survey and while they accounted for most of the hired workers, trends in labour use on smaller farms might have been different. For these reasons, changes in labour use as revealed in the farm survey were not expected to mirror those shown by the parish statistics.

4.1 Analysis of parish statistics

Between 1960 and 1960 the hired farm labour force in England and Wales decreased by 37.1 per cent, in the eastern region by 36.7 per cent. Net losses in the Haverhill and Stevenage areas were slightly larger, 39.8 per cent and 40.5 per cent respectively, but Cambridge losses (31.1 per cent) were smaller than the national or regional average.

Parishes near Cambridge lost considerably fewer workers than the more distant Fen parishes, repeating the trend observed throughout the larger Cambridge sub-region. As Appendix Table A4.1 shows, this was consistent for every category of labour in the sub-region and for most categories in the survey area. For Haverhill the position was reversed with a heavier net loss of workers from farms close to the town; this held for most categories individually. In the Stevenage area the pattern was less clear but the net result was a somewhat smaller reduction in hired labour from farms in parishes near the town.

4.2 Changes in labour on survey farms

Farms farthest from Cambridge lost a much larger proportion of their regular workers than farms close to the city, the middle farms being between the two extremes. Losses from farms near and farther from Haverhill and Stevenage were all of the same order, between 33 per cent and 38 per cent, and showed no definite trend according to distance from the centres.

Comparisons of numbers of workers between two dates reveal net changes in employment. The net changes may, however, conceal gross inflows and outflows of labour several times larger. One measure of gross change is the distribution of the labour force by length of service, a high proportion of newcomers indicating a rapid turnover of labour. On this measure, mobility appears to have been greater on farms nearer the towns. In each area the farms near the town had recruited more workers within the last two or the last five years while the farms farther away tended to have more long serving workers. Surprisingly, however, farms near Stevenage had more workers who had been in the same jobs for twenty years or more as well as more recent recruits, than farms farther from the town. (Appendix Table A4.2).

As shown in the table, 22 per cent of regular hired workers for England and Wales as a whole had been on the same farms for twenty years or longer. Most groups of farms in the survey had a larger proportion of long serving workers. The Haverhill sample demonstrated this tendency most clearly, 38 per cent of workers having been in the same jobs for twenty years or more. This has obvious implications for mobility and replacement of the labour force.

To summarise, while labour turnover was higher near the towns, the net reduction in the farm labour supply was generally greater from the more rural parishes. Only in the Haverhill area was the net outflow of workers heavier from farms near the town than from more distant farms.

5. Alternative sources of labour

Farmers faced with a dwindling supply of regular labour have several courses open to them. Through increased mechanisation, improved buildings and other means they may substitute capital for labour and so avoid having to replace workers who leave. They may change the system of farming, perhaps replacing a labour intensive livestock enterprise with another less demanding in labour, or by growing less roots and more cereals, cut down their annual labour requirements. Streamlining or simplifying work routines may save many man hours. Alternatively they may make greater use of other kinds of labour. This chapter discusses the substitution of family labour, seasonal labour and agricultural contractors for regular workers and, for the latter two categories of labour, considers the effects of proximity to towns on their availability and use.

5.1 Farm family labour

As hired workers leave the land, dependence on farmers and members of their families will increase. The contribution of the farm family, including farmers themselves, to the regular labour force on farms in the Haverhill survey increased from 28 per cent to 38 per cent over the ten years, similarly from 28 per cent to 38 per cent on Stevenage farms and from 30 per cent to 34 per cent on Cambridge farms. There was an *absolute* as well as a relative increase in the farm family contribution, of the order of 3 per cent for each group of farms, suggesting that as holdings are amalgamated, more sons and brothers are drawn into partnership or directorships in the family business. The substitution of farm family for hired workers has far reaching consequences for the future development of farming. The situation may soon be reached in the eastern region, as is already the case elsewhere, in which the farmer with his family performs a larger share of the farm work than the hired labour force.

5.2 Seasonal labour

Use of seasonal labour will reflect the interaction of demand and supply. Demand will vary with the season and the type of farming. Fen farmers have in the past relied heavily on seasonal labour for hoeing sugar beet and harvesting potatoes and onions and for the production of field vegetables, market garden and glasshouse crops. The middle Cambridge area in the survey has a large and expanding acreage of top fruit. Near Cambridge and in the Stevenage area, farming is more varied and casual labour is required for horticultural crops, haymaking and corn harvest, picking Brussels sprouts and plucking turkeys. (No information was collected on the use of seasonal labour on Haverhill farms).

The potential supply of seasonal labour may vary according to factors like the type of work to be performed, population density, alternative employment available, the level of household incomes and social class. In the Fens, farmers employ gang labour for hoeing sugar beet and lifting potatoes where a gang might consist of housewives, Irish labourers or 'van dwellers' (gypsies). Stevenage farms and those near Cambridge make use of a wide variety of workers including students at harvest and school children at weekends. Some Stevenage farmers employ shift workers from the factories and others with unusual working hours, such as postmen and railwaymen, who might have free afternoons. Table 5.1 indicates the number of farmers using each type of worker but not numbers of workers involved; gangs on Fen farms might consist of ten or twenty workers while tasks like bale carting might only involve one or two extra workers.

Employment of seasonal workers is generally decreasing, with some shift from males to females. Appendix Table A4.1 showed that the reduction in seasonal workers was heavier near each of the towns in the survey than from more rural areas but

33

Table 5.1   Types of seasonal and casual workers employed on survey farms

| | Stevenage | Cambridge | |
		Near	Middle and Far
	number of farms using this type of worker		
Housewives	15	2	33
School children	28	3	5
Students	12	6	—
Pensioners	6	2	5
Van dwellers	2	3	22
Irishmen	1	3	—
Gang labour	—	2	14
Factory workers	11	—	—
Other urban workers	17	2	—
Farm workers	3	—	3
Neighbours, relatives	—	1	1

conversely, Appendix Table A5.1 shows that parishes accessible to towns in the Cambridge sub-region lost only half as many seasonal workers as the more remote parishes. This tendency for losses to be heavier in the more rural areas held for each town individually (Except Haverhill) and for adult males, youths and females separately. The small net reduction in female seasonal labour near towns in the sub-region compared with the more rural parishes was particularly striking.

When farmers in the survey were asked if they had changed the use of seasonal labour over the decade, the majority in the Stevenage area thought they had not changed while more decreases than increases were reported in the Cambridge area. Increases outnumbered decreases on farms near Stevenage but decreases were more likely in the outer Stevenage area and particularly so for farms near Cambridge (Table 5.2).

It seems probable that in the survey areas, changes in demand were more influential than changes in supply accounting for the decreasing use of seasonal labour. Sugar beet is widely grown in these areas and accounts for much of the seasonal labour employed at the time of the agricultural census.

34

Table 5.2   Change in use of seasonal labour on survey farms 1961–2 to 1971–2

	Increase	No change	Decrease	All farms	Numbers
	per cent of farms				
Stevenage:					
near	32.4	41.1	26.5	100.0	34
far	22.9	48.5	28.6	100.0	35
total	27.5	45.0	27.5	100.0	69
Cambridge:					
near	17.0	28.0	55.0	100.0	29
middle	35.0	30.0	35.0	100.0	37
far	25.0	34.0	41.0	100.0	32
total	26.5	31.7	41.8	100.0	98

Use of monogerm seed, precision drilling and pre-emergence weed control have reduced the need for hand labour considerably. Some farmers now find it is only necessary to hand hoe the beet crop once in the season instead of four times as before. Similarly in the case of potatoes and onions, advances in mechanisation are reducing the demand for hand labour. Increasing emphasis on seasonal labour in accessible parishes of the Cambridge sub-region relative to remote parishes is consistent with a growing concentration of horticultural crops and hence an increasing demand for seasonal labour near the towns.

Evidence from elsewhere suggests that availability of other employment will reduce the supply of seasonal labour for agriculture. Pembrokeshire farmers growing early potatoes and vegetables have found that women who were accustomed to work on these crops no longer come because their husbands have found better paid jobs in new industries or because they themselves have taken full time jobs in the towns (*Farmers Weekly*, 1973c). Scottish farmers anticipate that fewer women will be willing to come and harvest potatoes or to pick raspberries because their husbands will be earning high wages in industry or with the oil companies (*Farmers Weekly*, 1973a).

The majority of farmers interviewed had not encountered difficulty in hiring seasonal labour. As Table 5.3 shows, farmers in the middle Cambridge area were the most likely to complain of shortages. This was the area experiencing the most rapid increase in demand for seasonal workers due to the expansion of orchards. Very few farmers near Stevenage, compared with those at a distance, reported any problems in hiring seasonal workers.

Table 5.3   Difficulty in obtaining seasonal labour on survey farms

	Difficult	Not difficult	No reply or do not know	All farms	Numbers
		per cent of farms			
Stevenage:					
near	4.5	72.8	22.7	100.0	44
far	24.1	48.1	27.8	100.0	54
total	15.3	59.2	25.5	100.0	98
Cambridge:					
near	31.0	48.3	20.7	100.0	98
middle	46.0	51.3	2.7	100.0	37
far	25.0	71.9	3.1	100.0	32
total	34.6	57.1	8.3	100.0	98

It seems likely that proximity to a town increases the potential supply of seasonal workers because it is town rather than country housewives who are employed. Women with small children may be unable to take regular jobs in shops, factories or offices but may be prepared to work temporarily on the land, bringing the children with them. In the Vale of Evesham, for instance, farmers and growers were able to employ women from town housing estates for fruit picking. Both the pay and change of scene were welcome to town housewives whereas country women seemed to prefer regular employment in factories to land work (Woods, 1968). It has been reported than one leading Kent fruit grower prefers to recruit and train women with no previous experience of strawberry picking in order to maintain high picking standards and therefore recruits housewives from local commuter estates (*Farmers Weekly*, 1973b). Fruit growers in the south east have claimed that the presence of a local industry is advantageous, particularly where workers' wives and men on shift work or on holiday are looking for some extra income (Gardner and Nicholson, 1974).

5.3 Agricultural contractors

Agricultural contractors might also be used to compensate for the loss of regular farm workers. While most farmers would hire contractors for construction work and jobs like field drainage or aerial spraying, needing specialised equipment, smaller farmers tend to employ them on a regular basis for those tasks requiring equipment which their small acreage does not justify owning, such as precision drilling, combining or baling, while larger farmers possessing the necessary machinery may call on contractors occasionally to help with routine work like ploughing or combing in a difficult season. The function of the contractor on the smaller farm is mainly to provide a specialised service, on the larger farm to supplement the regular labour force. Rather more farmers had increased than decreased the use of contractors over the survey period but the majority had not changed. Increase or decrease in use of contractors and of seasonal labour tended to go together.

Very few farmers in the survey reported any difficulty in finding contractors, the general view being that there were plenty available. Agricultural contractors were used less frequently on farms nearer towns than in the more rural areas (Table 5.4). This may be related to the fact that horticultural businesses, more commonly encountered near towns, rarely call on the services of agricultural contractors. Farmers near the towns were more likely than the rest to have reduced their reliance on contractors over the ten years, which might be a function of the heavier losses of regular labour from farms in the remoter areas.

Table 5.4　　　Change in use of agricultural contractors on survey farms

	Increase	Non-user or no change	Decrease	All farms	Numbers
		per cent of farms			
Stevenage:					
near	20.5	65.8	13.7	100.0	44
far	18.5	75.9	5.6	100.0	54
total	19.4	71.4	9.2	100.0	98
Cambridge:					
near	20.7	55.2	24.1	100.0	29
middle	13.5	64.8	21.7	100.0	37
far	34.4	53.1	12.5	100.0	32
total	22.4	58.2	19.4	100.0	98

Although there was apparently no dearth of contractors in the survey area despite the growth of the towns, farmers in other parts of the country are facing shortages. Pembrokeshire growers were losing not only their seasonal workers but also the services of haulage contractors as a result of industrial development. Scottish farmers affected by the North Sea oil boom are finding that building contractors are no longer available.

To summarise, it was suggested that farmers losing regular workers might be turning to alternative sources of labour. Farms in the survey showed increasing reliance on farm family labour and a slight increase in use of agricultural contractors but declining use of seasonal labour. There was no evidence that urban competition was seriously depleting the supply of seasonal workers or contractors. Agricultural contractors were readily available throughout the survey area irrespective of proximity of towns, although farmers in more rural areas seemed to be making greater use of them. Seasonal labour was generally available where there was a demand for it. Farmers near towns may have an advantage over those in more rural areas in recruiting seasonal workers. Industry may hasten the withdrawal of regular labour from farms but the wives of industrial workers may provide a pool of seasonal labour for nearby farms.

6. Reasons for leaving farms

The next two chapters deal with workers leaving farms, the means by which mobility is brought about and the influence of towns on migration from agriculture. The present chapter considers reasons for moving, and the next the jobs taken by those leaving farms. Reference is made to other studies in an attempt to build up a picture of the processes involved in 'the drift from the land.'

6.1 Reliability of information

Information was obtained by asking farmers why workers had left their employment over the previous ten years. In any survey which attempts to collect subjective information in a single interview there is a possibility that bias will be introduced through incomplete recall, deliberate withholding of information and through respondents rationalising past actions. In addition, objections are sometimes levelled against the principle of approaching employers rather than employees. Critics of this approach suggest it is essential to interview the workers themselves to discover the 'true' reasons behind a move since farmers may not be told the correct reasons or, if aware of the reasons, would be unlikely to disclose them.

Collecting information from farmers rather than workers can be justified in the present survey. In practical terms it is much easier to interview a hundred farmers in a locality than to search for several hundred of their ex-employees, some of whom will have left the district or perhaps changed jobs several times. The case for approaching workers instead of farmers was not convincing enough to justify a more elaborate survey procedure. Although it was suggested that farmers would be unlikely to know the 'true' reasons for workers leaving, in the face-to-face situation typical of farming, where a farmer knows his few employees well and probably works alongside them, it would be surprising if he did not gain an insight into their aspirations and grievances. In any case, moves due to straightforward reasons like further education or retirement can be reported objectively by employers as well as by workers. It was suggested, too, that farmers would not disclose the reasons for workers leaving even if they knew them. While it seems unlikely that farmers would admit to having lost workers through their shortcomings as employers, it seems equally unlikely that workers would admit blame on their part. If all decisions to leave agriculture originated with workers, a stronger case could be made for interviewing workers rather than farmers. Since, however, a contract of employment involves employer and worker alike, it can be terminated by either party. In the cases where the farmer takes the initiative the worker might not be in possession of the 'true' facts. Moreover, any bias introduced by the chosen survey method would be unlikely to affect the validity of comparisons made between workers leaving farms near and farther from towns.

6.2 Reasons for leaving farms

Most studies have emphasized the importance of low wages in accounting for 'the drift from the land' (see, for example, Orwin, 1938; Pedley, 1942; Cowie and Giles, 1957; Krier, 1961, 16; McIntosh, 1972). After low wages, workers leaving Gloucestershire farms mentioned long and uncertain hours of work, health, redundancy, working conditions and the tied cottage system (Cowie and Giles, 1957). C. S. Orwin believed inferior housing, lack of leisure and little opportunity for advancement were also of serious concern but W. H. Pedley considered that other drawbacks of the farm worker's life were subsidiary and would be removed if wages were improved.

Although wages were important, they did not appear to dominate the reasons for workers leaving farms in the eastern counties. Redundancy was the main reason for migration from Norfolk farms, accounting for 32.3 per cent of all moves. Wages came next (23.3 per cent) followed by dissatisfaction with work and conditions of employment (18.0 per cent), no other factor being of comparable importance (Wallace and Drudy, 1972).

Retirement was the most important single reason for workers leaving farms in the present survey. In order to compare these results with those of other studies it is necessary to consider only 'controllable' losses of workers, excluding moves due to unavoidable causes like age, ill health or death. As Table 6.1 shows, money was the most important of the controllable reasons but only in the Cambridge area was it clearly more important than other classes of reasons. Personal or family reasons, dismissal, redundancy, moves for better prospects and dissatisfaction with farm work all carried similar weight. Stevenage workers were the most likely to leave in order to improve their prospects or for family and personal reasons. Redundancy was particularly significant in the Haverhill sample, dismissal for other reasons on Cambridge farms. Unavoidable moves for retirement, death or ill health occurred more frequently in the Haverhill and Cambridge areas where they accounted for more than a third of all workers leaving.

6.3 Classifying reasons for moving

When discussing 'the drift from the land' it is customary to distinguish between 'push' and 'pull'. 'Push' factors are pressures generated in agriculture mainly associated with substitution of capital for labour, which tends to reduce demand for manpower on farms. 'Pull' factors reflect demand for labour in other industries and are manifest in higher wages, shorter hours, better conditions, improved housing and other benefits of urban living. The pull of expanding opportunities outside agriculture is widely believed to be more influential, in advanced economies today, than the push of contracting opportunities and deteriorating incomes in agriculture, in causing workers to leave (International Labour Office, 1960). F. McIntosh concluded that pull factors were two or three times as important as push

Table 6.1   Reasons for workers leaving survey farms

Reason	Haverhill	Stevenage	Cambridge	All farms
	per cent of controllable moves			
More money	16.6	21.0	24.7	21.1
Better prospects	12.7	17.1	9.3	12.9
Dissatisfied w. farm work	16.6	7.4	14.4	12.7
Personal or family	7.0	24.4	15.0	15.8
Dismissed	10.8	10.2	21.1	14.4
Redundant	22.9	9.1	12.4	14.4
Other reasons	13.4	10.8	3.1	8.7
All controllable moves	100.0	100.0	100.0	100.0
Number of moves:				
Controllable	157	176	194	527
Unavoidable	59	44	102	205
All moves	216	220	296	732

for men and five or six times for youths leaving Scottish farms (McIntosh, 1972). On the other hand M. Black considered after a study of Yorkshire farms that redundancy , a push factor, must have been more influential than suggested by previous writers since farmers were employing fewer men with no apparent strain (Black, 1968) while C. E. Heath and M. C. Whitby contended that technological advance in agriculture had been the main reason for declining employment on the land (Heath and Whitby, 1969).

A measure of the strength of push from agriculture for the economy as a whole is the extent to which workers leaving farms are replaced when other labour is available. Using the Department of Employment and Productivity's data for inter-industry movements of labour in Great Britain, H. Wagstaff estimated that gross losses of workers from agriculture were roughly double the net losses. This means that only about half the workers leaving were replaced and implies that the forces of push and pull were approximately equal (Wagstaff, 1971).

While the push-pull model is convenient for some purposes, it does not adequately represent the complexity of the processes involved in the transfer of labour out of agriculture. Demands for labour in agriculture and other industries at the macro level are so closely related that it becomes meaningless to try to separate them. The model has been criticised at the individual level, too, as an inadequate reflection of the complex psychological forces at work (Taylor, 1969). It does not provide a satisfactory basis for classifying motives for migration. Low wages or inferior housing may serve to push workers off the land but at the same time, higher wages or better housing in other occupations can be said to exert a pull. If a worker is dismissed but subsequently replaced or if he is made redundant on one farm but finds work on another, it is difficult to fit the move into this theoretical framework. In practice the reasons given by workers for leaving farms may have little bearing on the underlying forces of push and pull. Redundancy, the main expression of the push, is often effected by farmers failing to replace workers who leave voluntarily, who are pulled from agriculture, rather than by direct dismissal.

Instead of pursuing the theme of push and pull, an attempt is made here to classify reasons for workers leaving farms according to the origins of the decision. Workers themselves may initiate a move, motivated by the attraction of higher wages, shorter hours or better prospects in another job or through dissatisfaction with some aspect of the present job such as money, hours, type of work or personal relations. Also in this category comes moves made for personal reasons not necessarily connected with the job such as dislike of the locality or preference for another area, availability of housing, access to a town, marriage or marital breakdown. A second category of moves are those initiated by employers, usually for redundancy or unsatisfactory work. In the third category are unavoidable reasons for leaving, principally retirement and death.

On this basis, moves initiated by workers formed the largest group in each of the survey areas but only in Stevenage did they account for more than half the total. Unavoidable moves were nearly as important for Haverhill and Cambridge workers. Comparisons with results of the Scottish study suggest that while moves initiated by farmers were of the same order of importance in both areas, moves initiated by workers were much more important in Scotland, unavoidable reasons much less so (Table 6.2). A difference in this direction, but not perhaps of such magnitude, would be expected in view of the high average age of farm workers in eastern England.

Table 6.2   Summary of reasons for workers leaving farms

	Haverhill	Stevenage	Cambridge	Scotland	
				Youths	Adults
	per cent of workers leaving				
Initiated by worker or own accord	38.4	55.9	41.6	77.6	69.8
Initiated by employer or dismissed	24.6	15.5	21.9	19.8	20.4
Unavoidable or retired, died, other	37.0	28.6	36.5	2.6	9.8
All reasons	100.0	100.0	100.0	100.0	100.0
Number of workers leaving	216	220	296	313	1390

Source: (Scotland) F. McIntosh, 1972

6.4 Age and reasons for leaving

Younger workers are more inclined to initiate a move from agriculture, older men more likely to be dismissed or obliged to leave for unavoidable reasons. Studies in Gloucestershire, Nottinghamshire and Scotland have shown that pay, long hours, working conditions and further education are most important to young workers, promotion prospects, provision of

45

accommodation and personal reasons for workers between 25 and 35, whose family responsibilities would probably be the most pressing, relations with employers for workers in mid-career and health, the state of the tied cottage and redundancy for older men (Cowie and Giles, 1957; Hawkesworth, 1971; McIntosh, 1972).

In most respects the findings of the present survey were similar, as Table 6.3 shows. Dissatisfaction with hours and conditions, moves to attend college, for promotion or to start farming independently were all most pronounced for young workers. Young men, too, were the most liable to be dismissed for unsatisfactory work. Housing and personal reasons for moving were most prevalent with workers between 25 and 45 and almost as important for those over 45. The possibility of being made redundant increased with age and inevitably, most losses for retirement, ill health, and death were for workers over 45. This survey differed from the others in one important respect, namely that while all the others found pay to be most significant for young workers, it was men between 25 and 45 from Stevenage farms and men over 45 from Cambridge farms who were the most likely to have left in search of higher earnings.

6.5 Job opportunities and reasons for leaving

Evidence to the Select Committee on Agriculture in 1968 suggested that the basic tendency was for agriculture to release labour as a result of increasing productivity but that external economic circumstances would exert a considerable influence by increasing or decreasing the rate of outflow in a particular year. K. A. H. Murray reached a similar conclusion from a study of trends in the farm labour supply before the second world war (Murray, 1939). If the pull of alternative opportunities can vary from one period to another it can also vary from one place to another. Economic pressures within agriculture to release labour

Table 6.3   Age and reasons for workers leaving survey farms

| | Haverhill and Stevenage | | | Cambridge | | |
	Under 25	25–44	45–64	Under 25	25–44	45–64
	per cent of controllable moves					
Money	20.8	25.5	10.0	26.7	22.9	31.0
Dissatisfied	11.1	5.3	5.0	16.3	14.3	10.3
Personal, family	12.5	28.7	25.0	12.8	18.6	17.3
Advancement	38.9	19.2	0.0	9.3	12.9	3.4
Dismissed	9.7	12.8	2.5	26.7	17.0	17.3
Redundant	7.0	8.5	57.5	8.2	14.3	20.7
All controllable moves	100.0	100.0	100.0	100.0	100.0	100.0
Numbers	72	94	40	86	70	29

could be experienced to a similar degree throughout the economy but the means by which this labour transfer is effected might vary according to the strength of demand for labour in non-farm occupations. K. Cowling has demonstrated that the level of unemployment in a region, reflecting demand for labour, exerts a significant influence on the rate of outflow of workers from agriculture (Cowling, 1969). In the present survey the amount of labour lost from each area was of the same order but the manner in which these reductions came about varied considerably from place to place.

Young workers may be influenced to a greater extent than adults by the availability of work in the locality. For some school leavers, employment in agriculture may be less a deliberate career choice than a stop gap until something better turns up or until they are old enough to drive, go to college or join the forces. In remoter rural areas, lack of adequate public transport to the towns may be a serious obstacle to occupational choice for those too young to drive or own a

47

vehicle. These young people may see little alternative to finding work in the rural area. S. Hale has described the difficulties facing school leavers in rural Herefordshire in their search for suitable employment (Hale, 1971). A survey of boys leaving secondary modern schools in Norfolk showed that while most of those who lived in market towns were able to find work in the home town or a nearby village, fewer than half those from villages found work near their homes. Rural employment opportunities were still more limited for grammar school leavers and particularly for girls (Green and Ayton, 1967). The alternatives for 15- or 16-year olds living in rural areas not easily accessible to a town may be to continue in full time education, leave home, make a long and costly journey to work each day or take whatever employment is available locally. The latter usually means working on the land and more than half the Norfolk village boys who found local jobs worked on farms. Understandably, many of these young people would leave agriculture if other work became available and many will have left before the age of 20.

6.6 Distance from towns and reasons for leaving farms

It was predicted that where alternative employment had recently become available, workers would be the main initiators of moves out of agriculture but that where there was little to draw workers away, farmers would play a more positive role in reducing the labour force. Following a period of rapid migration, farmers would have to compete with one another for labour and this would encourage greater mobility between farms. Where farms had been exposed to urban labour markets for longest, losses would be mainly due to natural wastage. It was therefore predicted that workers would be the main initiators of moves from agriculture on farms near Haverhill and in the Stevenage area, that farmers would be the main initiators from areas least affected by urban industrial growth, namely farthest from Haverhill and Cambridge, and that unavoidable reasons would predominate on farms with longest exposure to urban influence, that is near Cambridge.

Table 6.4   Reasons for leaving survey farms and distance from towns.

| | Haverhill | | Stevenage | | Cambridge | | |
	Near	Far	Near	Far	Near	Middle	Far
	per cent of workers leaving						
Money	23.8	5.1	12.0	20.3	8.6	25.3	16.8
Prospects	3.8	12.5	19.6	9.4	6.9	8.7	2.2
Dissatisfied	17.5	8.8	6.5	5.5	8.6	11.0	9.0
Personal, family	6.2	4.4	15.2	22.6	9.5	8.7	11.3
Redundant	8.8	21.3	7.6	7.0	5.2	11.0	9.0
Dismissed	12.5	5.2	8.7	7.8	15.5	11.0	14.6
Retired	12.5	22.8	17.4	10.2	34.5	12.2	22.5
Died or ill	6.2	9.6	8.7	5.5	8.6	11.0	12.4
Other reasons	8.7	10.3	4.3	11.7	2.6	1.1	2.2
Worker initiated	51.3	30.8	53.3	57.8	33.6	53.7	39.3
Farmer initiated	21.3	26.5	16.3	14.8	20.7	22.0	23.6
Unavoidable	27.4	42.7	30.4	27.4	45.7	24.3	37.1
All reasons	100.0	100.0	100.0	100.0	100.0	100.0	100.0
Number of workers	83	133	92	128	116	91	89

This was generally borne out in practice. Taking the outer Haverhill area to represent farms least affected by industrial growth, Table 6.4 shows that workers here were the most liable of any to be made redundant and that this area had the highest proportion of moves initiated by farmers. Workers on these farms were the least likely to move in search of more money or for personal reasons and were unlikely to be dismissed as unsatisfactory workers. Farms farthest from Cambridge shared some of these tendencies. This contrasts with the situation on farms near Haverhill, experiencing rapid growth in non-farm employment for the first time during the 1960s. Here the main

49

reason for leaving was to obtain more money. Many workers became dissatisfied with farm work at this time and others were dismissed because their frequent complaints about money and hours caused trouble at work. The sudden influx of industrial workers with higher incomes and a higher standard of living would generate dissatisfaction among the rural population and cause some workers to change jobs. Few workers here were made redundant or forced to leave for unavoidable reasons in comparison with the large number moving of their own accord. Similarly in the outer Stevenage and middle Cambridge areas, where alternative employment was becoming increasingly available to rural workers during the 1960s as a result of industrial expansion and improved private transport to the towns, a large proportion of moves was made for better wages or better prospects and relatively few for unavoidable causes.

Near Stevenage, where industrial work had been available to the rural workforce for a longer time, some different trends emerged. Here, employers who had already adjusted their farming systems to a smaller labour force would be inclined to resist further reductions, offering workers greater inducements to stay. Those remaining on farms would in any case include more who would place a higher value on the non-financial rewards of the job. Consequently the attractions of higher wages elsewhere, dissatisfaction with farm work and dismissal were less important than in areas at an earlier stage of industrial expansion; conversely, more moves here were attributable to employers or were inescapable. Near Stevenage the most important reason for workers moving was to improve prospects within agriculture which suggests that farmers were competing among themselves to attract workers. At the most advanced stage of urban development represented by farms near Cambridge, where workers had been exposed to other opportunities for longest, few moves were made to other occupations and there was little surplus labour to be made redundant. Here retirement was the main reason for leaving.

6.7 Access to towns and mobility of rural youth

Since young men are likely to leave farms of their own accord, it would be expected that there would be a heavy outflow of young workers from farms nearer towns. There workers would have many opportunities to compare their conditions of employment with those of non-farm workers and if they chose to work in the town, transport would not pose a problem. In the new and expanding towns, too, industrial employers would be likely to recruit school leavers rather than older men, to train as the future skilled labour force. For these reasons farms near the towns would be expected to lose more young workers than those further away. In the more rural areas where there would be less to attract workers from agriculture, farmers might be obliged to make some redundant or would allow the labour force to decline by not replacing workers who retire. This suggests that those leaving farms in the more rural areas would be predominantly older men. On the other hand it could be argued that since young people living near towns or coming from urban backgrounds have a wider choice of occupations open to them, fewer would be obliged to start work on farms against their inclination and fewer would therefore drop out when other jobs became available. Farms in more rural areas, recruiting from a captive group of young workers, would expect to suffer a larger turnover subsequently.

Evidence from the survey generally supports the first suggestion. Table 6.5 shows that there were more young workers among those leaving farms close to Stevenage and Cambridge than leaving distant farms, the latter losing relatively more in the 25–45 age range. Losses of older workers were not consistently heavier from the remoter farms, however. According to Appendix Table A4.1, farms in parishes near Haverhill and Stevenage lost more young workers during the 1960s than parishes farther from the towns, as expected in view of the recent growth of opportunities for young workers in those towns. The opposite was true of the Cambridge area, due perhaps to the longer time for which other opportunities had been available.

Table 6.5   Age of workers leaving survey farms and distance from towns.

| | Stevenage | | Cambridge | | |
	Near	Far	Near	Middle	Far
	per cent of workers leaving				
Under 25	24.1	17.4	27.8	42.8	21.6
25–44	37.9	55.6	23.5	28.6	29.6
45–64	20.7	17.4	13.9	15.4	26.1
65 and over	17.3	9.6	34.8	13.2	22.7
All workers leaving	100.0	100.0	100.0	100.0	100.0
Numbers	87	115	115	91	88

Earlier it was suggested that while pressures generated within agriculture to reduce the labour force would be experienced to a similar degree in all areas, the manner in which workers actually left farms would depend on the alternatives available. This chapter has demonstrated that the availability of other jobs affects the reasons given for workers leaving farms. This effect is not necessarily adverse to agriculture. From a north Wales study W. D. Jones concluded that in retrospect many farmers may have been grateful for construction schemes since their net effect was to reduce employment on farms which were previously overstaffed, with consequent improvements in farm income (Jones, 1972). A number of farmers in the present survey commented, too, that if workers had not left of their own accord, more would have been made redundant. This suggests that, rather than interfering with efficient farming, development of alternative employment may in fact assist farmers to make necessary reductions in the labour force.

7. Occupations of workers leaving farms

The previous chapter showed that the reasons given for workers leaving farms vary according to the availability of other jobs, the relationship between the local employment situation and the age at which workers move being rather more tenuous. Subsequent occupations of those leaving farms will also vary depending on what is available locally. This chapter discusses occupations taken by workers leaving farms, the relationships between occupation, age and reasons for leaving and traces the influence of industrial development on this pattern.

7.1 Typical occupations for ex-farm workers

By no means all workers moving from farms leave the agricultural industry. Many move to other farms where wages or conditions may be more favourable or where they may exercise their skills more fully, assume greater responsibility or gain promotion. Typically between 40 and 50 per cent of all moves are within agriculture (Black, 1968; Hawkesworth, 1971; McIntosh, 1972; Drudy and Wallace, 1972; Pickard, 1972). Others leaving farms move to closely related occupations in the agricultural industry. Workers who leave agriculture will be likely to take unskilled or semi-skilled manual jobs, for reasons previously discussed. Not all farming skills are readily transferable but driving heavy machinery or working on a construction site may not be unlike work on a modern arable farm and may for this reason serve to bridge the gap between farm and non-farm work. Motor transport, building and construction were popular alternatives for young workers contemplating a move from agriculture, and others who expected to move, but were undecided about their future occupation, said they would prefer another outdoor job (Bessell, 1972). Employment in a factory, confined to one place, indoors and in company with others would be an unfamiliar work situation for the farm worker and might be viewed unfavourably on that account.

In the survey 44 per cent of workers had moved to other farms or to related occupations such as agricultural contracting. About a quarter had taken other 'outdoor' jobs, often in rural areas, in building or construction, plant hire, drainage or haulage contracting or with local authorities or river boards. Only 22 per cent had gone into factories and the rest had moved to unskilled jobs, mainly in towns and often in retailing or other service occupations, referred to in Table 7.1 as 'urban' jobs.

Table 7.1   **Occupations of workers leaving survey farms**

	Haverhill	Stevenage	Cambridge	Total
Farm work	33	61	79	173
Farm related work	6	4	22	32
Building, construction	13	12	15	40
Driving	12	8	13	33
Plant hire, drainage	2	3	8	13
Local authority	6	10	13	29
Factory	41	40	23	104
Other urban, service	13	10	18	41
Housewife, student	17	13	5	35
No occupation	67	42	83	192
Not known	6	17	17	40
All workers leaving	216	220	296	732
		per cent gainfully employed		
Farm or related	31.0	43.6	52.8	44.0
'Outdoor' manual	26.2	22.2	25.7	24.7
Factory	32.5	26.8	12.1	22.3
'Urban'	10.3	7.4	9.4	9.0
All gainfully employed	100.0	100.0	100.0	100.0
Numbers employed	126	149	191	466

7.2 Age and other occupations

D. Pickard has distinguished two separate trends, one a movement of young workers between 18 and 24, mainly out of agriculture and the other of men between 25 and 29, largely between farms. The latter is the stage at which a trained and experienced man will move to better his prospects (Pickard, 1972). The Scottish and Nottinghamshire studies both suggested that youths are less committed to remaining in agriculture than men in the prime of their working lives but the present survey did not follow this trend. As Table 7.2 shows, the majority of workers in all age groups remained in agricultural employment and even among the under-25s, mobility was mainly between farms. In the Cambridge area a number of young men had left farms in order to set up on their own account as agricultural contractors. Other 'outdoor' manual jobs were generally preferred to work in manufacturing industry by men under 45. Work in factories appealed more to those over 45, some of whom were obliged by ill health to find lighter, indoor work.

Table 7.2   Occupations and ages of workers leaving survey farms.

Occupation	Haverhill and Stevenage			Cambridge		
	Under 25	25–44	45–64	Under 25	25–44	45–64
	per cent of workers gainfully employed					
Farm or related	39.2	40.4	41.2	47.4	59.4	43.6
'Outdoor' manual	21.6	26.6	11.8	31.5	20.3	28.2
Factory	27.4	24.5	41.2	13.2	10.9	15.4
'Urban'	11.8	8.5	5.8	7.9	9.4	12.8
All gainfully employed	100.0	100.0	100.0	100.0	100.0	100 0
Numbers	51	94	34	76	64	39

7.3   Reasons for moving and subsequent occupations

The Scottish survey showed that dismissed workers were more likely to find themselves other farm jobs while those leaving of their own accord were more inclined to move to the towns, a tendency more marked for youths than adults. In the present survey, dismissed workers were again more likely to move to other farms but here those initiating a move most often sought other 'outdoor' manual jobs.

Workers moving in order to earn more money were the least likely of any to stay in agriculture but surprisingly, a quarter of those leaving Cambridge farms for this reason stayed in agriculture. It is not unusual for young workers to move to larger farms in order to earn more overtime. Nearly half of those seeking higher wages chose 'outdoor' manual jobs like building and driving, especially in the Cambridge area. Haverhill and Stevenage workers leaving farms were more likely to go into factories in search of more money. Unskilled jobs in towns other than in manufacturing industry did not attract many of those desiring higher wages.

The majority of workers leaving for other reasons stayed in agriculture. Almost by definition, moves to enhance career prospects would be within the industry. More than a third of the workers dissatisfied with some aspect of the present farm job and more than half those moving for family or personal reasons stayed on farms, other 'outdoor' manual jobs being next choice for both groups. Workers made redundant usually found work on other farms, those dismissed for other reasons being more inclined to take non-farm jobs. About half the workers obliged to leave farms through ill health or injury eventually returned to agriculture but many took lighter jobs as caretakers, van drivers or gardeners, usually in towns (Table 7.3).

The results of this survey are unusual in certain respects, compared with other similar surveys. Money was less important among the reasons for leaving farms in this study, younger workers were not the most likely to leave in search of better wages, younger men who changed jobs were more inclined to remain in agriculture and even some of those motivated to increase their earnings went to other farms. The level of non-farm earnings in the region and the structure of earnings on

Table 7.3   Reasons for leaving survey farms and occupations taken.

Reason	Farm	'Outdoor'	Factory	'Urban'	Total	Numbers
		per cent of gainful occupations				
Money	11.8	48.2	36.4	3.6	100.0	110
Dissatisfied	37.5	31.3	17.2	14.0	100.0	64
Personal, family	52.2	23.9	17.9	6.0	100.0	67
Advancement	86.7	6.7	2.2	4.4	100.0	45
Redundant	60.6	14.3	19.7	5.4	100.0	56
Dismissed	37.5	28.6	26.8	7.1	100.0	56
Unavoidable	52.5	10.0	10.0	27.5	100.0	40
All reasons	44.0	24.7	22.3	9.0	100.0	438

farms may each contribute to the explanation. During the period of the survey, average weekly earnings of manual workers in East Anglia were lower than in any other region of Great Britain so that moving from agriculture to another industry was less remunerative than elsewhere. Although average earnings on farms were also low they would vary considerably according to farm size. On a large farm a young, energetic worker might be able to increase his income substantially by working overtime. On a large farm, too, there is some chance of promotion, on a small farm virtually none. The ambitious young worker in the eastern region might therefore stand to increase his earnings more by moving within agriculture than by going to an unskilled non-farm job.

7.4 Influence of the local employment pattern

Other occupations taken by ex-farm workers will reflect what is available locally. Rapid industrial growth in the Stevenage and Haverhill areas during the period under study would suggest that most workers leaving farms there would have moved to industry. Since manufacturing was less dominant in the Cambridge area and since employment was not expanding as rapidly during the 1960s, it was expected that fewer workers from that area would have moved to factories, more to other

57

jobs like building and transport. As Table 7.1 indicated, this was partly true, one third of the workers from Haverhill farms and one quarter from Stevenage taking jobs in factories compared with only one in eight from Cambridge farms. More than half the Cambridge workers went on other farms or to related agricultural occupations. Numbers choosing 'outdoor' manual work or 'urban' jobs other than in factories differed little between the three areas.

Despite the emphasis on manufacturing employment in Haverhill and Stevenage, surprisingly few workers leaving farms in these areas went to work in the factories. One reason is that new jobs in manufacturing industry and accompanying new housing would be reserved in the first place for the overspill population. Growth of the towns themselves and the increase in population would, however, generate much new employment in local firms, for example in building and other services, and this would be open to local workers. A census of Haverhill in 1966 showed that only about half the workers coming from the town itself or from other parts of East Anglia worked in factories compared with 72 per cent of ex-Londoners (West Suffolk County Council, 1968). Networks of information about job vacancies, the policy of allocating new houses to Londoners and the adjustment process for the individual could all predispose those leaving agriculture to seek predominantly outdoor manual types of employment.

7.5 Other occupations and access to towns

Assuming that most workers leaving farms seek employment locally, those living near towns can choose between urban and rural jobs while those living in remoter areas have a narrower choice. Consequently it was predicted that workers leaving farms nearer towns would be more likely than those from more rural areas to take urban and industrial jobs. Table 7.4 shows, however, that this was only true of the Haverhill sample. Twice as many workers leaving farms near the town had moved straight to factories while nearly twice as many from the more rural area had gone to other farms. For Stevenage there was little difference in respect of other jobs between workers from inner and outer parishes; in fact slightly more leaving farms near the town had gone to other farms or to 'outdoor' manual jobs which might be in rural areas, rather more from the less accessible farms to factories or other jobs in the town. In the case of Cambridge, it was the farms farthest from the city which had lost most workers to factories and fewest to other farms. Workers moving from farms near the city were the most likely to go to other farms, while from the middle area many had chosen related occupations like agricultural contracting. Similar proportions from each area had taken other kinds of 'outdoor' or 'urban' unskilled jobs, some Fen farm workers becoming lorry drivers, more living near Cambridge becoming college porters or gardeners.

Table 7.4   Occupations of workers leaving survey farms and distance from towns.

| | Haverhill | | Stevenage | | Cambridge | | |
	Near	Far	Near	Far	Near	Middle	Far
	per cent gainfully employed						
Farm or related	22.6	39.1	44.8	42.9	56.5	59.7	41.9
'Outdoor'	25.8	26.5	27.6	18.6	17.7	31.3	27.4
Factory	43.5	21.9	25.9	27.5	8.1	6.0	22.6
'Urban'	8.1	12.5	1.7	11.0	17.7	3.0	8.1
All gainfully employed	100.0	100.0	100.0	100.0	100.0	100.0	100.0
Numbers	62	64	58	91	62	67	62

In short, the relationship between accessibility to non-farm employment and the pattern of occupations taken by workers leaving farms was as anticipated for Haverhill, non-existent for Stevenage and reversed for Cambridge. The explanation may lie in the fact that non-farm employment has been available in

59

these areas for varying amounts of time. Bishop suggested that the lag in migration from the remote areas would be related to the extent of industrial development, the location of industry and social and cultural differences among the population. Discounting social and cultural differences in the present context, it seems likely that rates of migration from farms would be affected by *location* or distance from an employment centre and *extent of industrial development*, depending on the length of time for which industry has been established at that location. Since the survey areas represent different stages in the process of industrial development, with Haverhill the most recent and Cambridge the longest established and since the effect of distance from towns has also been taken into account, the results of the survey may be used to illustrate successive stages in the adjustment process.

Haverhill's development was the most recent and it seems probable that during the 1960s the main impact of industrial growth would have been felt in the town itself and in villages and farms within a limited radius. Here a large proportion of the potentially mobile workers left agriculture for jobs in the town, often in factories. Industrial employers would be recruiting the greater part of their labour in this period and farmers might lose a number of workers in quick succession. Few workers at this stage were moving between farms.

Stevenage began to industrialise ten years earlier and as the rate of economic growth was higher, it seems likely that the influence of employment in the new town had already been felt throughout the area covered by the survey. Potentially mobile workers would have had an opportunity to leave agriculture during the 1950s when firms would have been recruiting the bulk of their workers and most changes in farm organisation may have occurred at that time. Demands from industry might have slackened to some extent after the first ten years but with fewer workers remaining in agriculture there might be stronger competition between farms for workers. Farmers might offer certain concessions to attract and retain workers and this might

60

encourage them to move between farms more freely than before.

Development of industry during the 1960s would not be likely to have had a marked impact on agricultural employment in the Cambridge area. Workers on farms easily accessible to the city would have been exposed to alternative opportunities for long enough that those wishing to move could already have done so. Those remaining on farms therefore did so largely by choice or because their mobility was in some way restricted. As in the Stevenage area, most moves were between farms.

Farms in the areas least affected by alternative employment, represented by the outer Haverhill and Cambridge areas, illustrated the situation where urban influence was only beginning to be felt. Although the majority of moves were between farms, the least satisfied workers were beginning to leave in search of other opportunities. In the Haverhill area, the new factories in Haverhill and surrounding villages and increased activity in building and haulage firms would serve to attract some workers from the less accessible farms. A number of Fen farm workers from the outer Cambridge area had also moved to factory jobs. Here it was improved personal mobility rather than local development of industry which had triggered off the exodus. At least one Cambridge firm had started running a bus to the area to collect workers but most of the ex-farm workers were driving daily to work in Newmarket factories, a distance of some fifteen miles, with several sharing a car. The East Anglia Economic Planning Council (1968) noted that journeys to work from the Isle of Ely to towns like Cambridge and Peterborough had increased noticeably in the 1950s and 1960s and that distances travelled often exceeded twenty miles each way. Although the majority of journeys to work in the region are of less than seven miles, it is clear that some workers are prepared to travel much greater distances if no suitable work is available locally.

If this synthesis is realistic it should follow that the greatest changes will occur in future in the remoter rural areas with a surplus agricultural population. In areas which have been exposed to alternative employment for some time, an increasing proportion of all job changes will be within agriculture, with fewer workers leaving farms for other industries.

8. Conditions of employment on farms

The third question to be answered in this study was how the growth of towns, provision of alternative employment in rural areas and migration from the land affect workers who remain on farms. Findings of the survey so far suggest that while growth of new jobs in the locality encourages rapid migration from farms for a few years, the farm labour force soon regains its equilibrium. On farms near Stevenage and more notably near Cambridge, where other employment had been available for longest, relatively few workers were leaving farms for more money or because they were dissatisfied with farm work. Few moved into industry, more went to other farms. One explanation is that potentially mobile and dissatisfied workers would have left earlier and hence that those remaining would be less mobile, whether by choice or personal constraints on their movement. Another possibility, raised by other studies, is that access to towns is regarded favourably by workers and their families, and that this helps to stabilise the labour force. A third suggestion is that farmers who have already lost workers to other industries will be obliged to improve conditions of employment if they are to hold the remaining workers and compete with other farmers for the dwindling supply of labour. All three explanations may be valid. This chapter develops the suggestion that earnings and conditions of employment will be more favourable on farms near towns while the next considers the effects of proximity to towns on the lives of farm workers and their families.

8.1 Earnings

At the time the survey was completed the statutory minimum wage for an adult full time male farm worker in England and Wales was £16.20 for a 42-hour week. The wages structure which provides premiums for craftsmen, supervisors and managers had not been introduced but nevertheless most workers at that time were receiving more than the minimum wage. For England and Wales as a whole, weekly earnings in 1972 averaged £23.67, basic earnings being supplemented by overtime, piecework, bonuses, other agreed premiums and payments in kind.

Farmers in the survey were asked about earnings, perquisites and housing of present workers. It should not be inferred from this that workers leaving farms had received the same treatment. Their leaving might have spurred farmers on to improve wages and conditions for those remaining or farmers might have discriminated in their treatment in favour of workers whom they wished to retain. Cambridge farmers were asked for more detailed information about the methods of supplementing workers' earnings. Some volunteered the amounts paid as premiums or supplied details of gross annual earnings or take home pay. This information was not always forthcoming and it is possible that the response was biased towards those who paid more.

A premium agreed between farmer and worker proved to be the most usual form of supplementing wages. Premiums are the amounts by which total earnings exceed the wage prescribed by Agricultural Wages Board Order for total hours worked. Workers are, of course, entitled to statutory rates for overtime hours but some employers made a conscious policy of offering unlimited overtime, providing workers an opportunity to supplement their earnings substantially. Others guaranteed payment for a minimum amount of overtime each week regardless of whether these hours were actually worked. Some employers paid bonuses on production or made presentations at harvest or Christmas and a few ran private pension schemes. In

64

some cases workers earned piecework rates for singling sugar beet, in others the employer paid the worker's income tax and his national insurance contribution.

Nearly all workers in the survey were earning more than the statutory minimum wage. Those few receiving only the basic wage were usually sons of farmers who would eventually become partners in the business, youths not yet very skilled or experienced, older workers with no particular skill or responsibility, workers on unprofitable small farms. Some with small holdings of their own worked only the basic hours in return for the minimum wage but were permitted to borrow machinery and implements or received other forms of practical assistance from their employers.

It was expected that farmers near towns would be under greater pressure to pay rates above the minimum. Those feeling themselves to be protected from industrial competition by distance, or who still had surplus labour on their farms, would have less incentive to raise wages. As Bishop observed, in advanced economies today the highest rates of migration are occurring from remote agricultural areas characterised by low returns to farm labour (Bishop, 1965). Evidence was found to support this suggestion at both the regional and the local level.

During most of the nineteenth century farmers in Britain could employ as much labour as they wished at rates of pay below those common in towns, average rates in each district being set roughly by distance from urban centres where there was other work. At the turn of the century average weekly cash earnings of farm workers in the east, West Midlands and south of England were considerably below rates in the industrial north (Whetham, 1960, 104–116). To some extent these differences persist. Although farms in the eastern counties were paying the highest rates during the 1930s (Pedley, 1942), today agricultural earnings in the more industrialised East Midlands and south east are well above those of the south west or eastern region. The Wages and Employment Enquiry showed average weekly earnings and hourly rates to be lowest in the eastern region and the *Farmers Weekly* survey of farm workers' earnings illustrated the regional differences still more clearly (Ministry of Agriculture, Fisheries and Food, 1973; Butcher, 1972).

The low earnings of farm workers in the eastern region cannot be attributed to the nature of the labour force. Although farmers in this region employ fewer workers in the high paid categories of dairy cowmen and stockmen, relatively more of the lower paid general farm workers. East Anglia has more large farms than the other regions and earnings are higher on larger farms. Newby suggested that isolation from labour markets is still a potent cause of low earnings among agricultural workers. Comparative isolation of farms in the past and the nature of individual bargaining between each farmer and his employees resulted in a wide dispersal of earnings about the average in each region or county. Although the Agricultural Wages Board has enforced a national minimum wage since 1942, local custom still dictates to some extent the incidence and level of additional payments. The keener the competition for labour in each district, the more likely that farmers will offer rates above the minimum so that 'local custom' is eroded and each farmer strives to compete with other farmers and with industrial employers (Newby, 1972a). A recent survey has shown, for example, that half the regular farm workers in the Slough-Hillingdon area were being paid more than £2.00 above the basic rate because of competition with the relatively high wages paid in the towns (Agricultural Development and Advisory Service, 1973).

In each of the survey areas the payment of premiums was more widespread on farms nearer the town, as seen in Table 8.1. The fact that average amounts paid always appeared higher on the less accessible farms might be related to provision of housing, a point which will be discussed later. Although these averages were based on a small number of cases and, as suggested earlier, these might be a biased sample, it is worth noting that the average premium for full time male farm workers in England and Wales in 1971 was nearly £3.00 a week, considerably more than the amount offered on Haverhill and Cambridge farms. This supports the view that East Anglian farm workers are not well paid. Premiums were generally higher on Stevenage farms and there is a tradition for farm workers to migrate from the more rural counties of Norfolk and Suffolk to higher paid jobs on Hertfordshire farms.

Table 8.1   **Payment of premiums and distance from towns.**

	Farmers with full time workers paying premiums	Full time hired workers receiving	Mean amount per week
	per cent	per cent	£
Haverhill			
near	93.5	95.2	1.50
far	85.7	89.0	1.70
Stevenage			
near	100.0	99.0	3.70
far	92.5	96.0	4.60
Cambridge			
city	100.0	100.0	1.90
near	86.5	90.2	1.90
middle	78.2	88.5	1.80
far	60.8	82.5	2.40

Payment of premiums depends to some extent on access to an urban labour market and there was evidence from the Cambridge survey that payment of other benefits is also influenced by distance from the city. Table 8.2 shows that pension schemes were encountered only in the more urbanised parishes with more than half the workers on farms near the city included, compared with less than one fifth in the middle area and none in the most rural area. About one third of the workers on farms near the city and two thirds in the middle area had the opportunity to work unlimited overtime but this was rarely mentioned in the more rural district. Payment of the worker's income tax and insurance stamp was only found in the Fens.

Table 8.2   Type of benefits paid and distance from Cambridge.

	Farmers with hired workers paying benefits			Hired workers benefitting		
	Near	Middle	Far	Near	Middle	Far
	per cent			per cent		
Premium	88.0	64.3	62.5	95.5	83.3	85.0
Unlimited overtime	20.0	32.2	8.3	33.1	64.2	7.5
Pension	20.0	3.6	0.0	55.0	19.0	0.0
Bonus	12.0	10.7	0.0	1.8	11.0	0.0
Stamp, tax paid	0.0	10.7	12.5	0.0	2.2	5.4
Total farms or workers	25	28	24	218	137	93

8.2 Perquisites

Perquisites available to workers will depend on the type of farming. More than half the workers on farms in the Cambridge survey, for example, were entitled to take potatoes and nearly half were offered other vegetables or fruit and had the right to collect firewood. According to the farmers workers did not often avail themselves of these perquisites. Milk and eggs were not often produced on these predominantly arable farms but some Stevenage farmers provided milk, poultry or eggs. On vegetable growing farms workers sometimes had the option of buying produce at cost price, the employers preferring not to make free gifts of produce. In Cambridgeshire and particularly in the Fens it is still customary for farm workers to rent smallholdings which they work in their spare time. Farmers here sometimes provided surplus seed or fertiliser or loaned tractors, machinery or vehicles for use on the worker's holding. Three large farms near Cambridge provided protective clothing for their employees but this was not a general practice in the area.

In the Stevenage area almost all perquisites were supplied by more farmers and available to more workers on farms near the town than farther away. This implies that perquisites may be used as a means of attracting or holding workers in areas more vulnerable to competition for labour. In the Cambridge area the evidence suggested that workers near the city were being treated as far as possible like those in any other industry while in the Fens, labour management followed more traditional lines. Workers in the most rural area were the most likely to receive the traditional types of benefit, almost all being supplied with free potatoes and many with free vegetables and fruit. Here, too, many workers were given various kinds of assistance with their smallholdings. On farms near Cambridge free supplies of potatoes, vegetables or firewood were less forthcoming but more workers were given the option of buying produce cheaply and, like industrial workers, might have protective clothing provided. Near Cambridge, too, workers more often had the opportunity of participating in the firm's pension scheme and of working overtime at their own discretion. As Table 8.3 shows, the middle area combined both approaches with a wide variety of concessions offered. Some workers were supplied with free produce and firewood but others had the option of buying produce at the packhouse. The forms of supplementing wages also varied widely, some workers earning production bonuses, some joining pension schemes and others having the chance to work unlimited overtime.

8.3 Housing

The Agricultural Wages Board prescribes the value of cottages, board and lodging and milk which may legally be deducted from wages. Since these allowable charges are lower than market values and since some farmers do not even deduct the nominal charges, the real value of payments in kind represents a subsidy to the farm worker. The tied cottage is the most substantial form of subsidy. At the time of the survey cottages were officially valued at 30p. per week and it has been estimated that rent is deducted for only about half the tied cottages in the country (Giles and Cowie, 1961).

Table 8.3   Perquisites available on survey farms and distance from towns.

Stevenage:	Farms supplying perquisites		Hired workers receiving	
	Near	Far	Near	Far
	per cent		per cent	
Firewood	23.3	14.3	32.8	29.7
Potatoes	20.0	11.4	29.0	19.8
Milk	13.3	11.4	15.9	14.4
Eggs	13.3	11.4	16.8	5.4
Poultry	3.3	5.7	12.2	7.2
Brussels sprouts	0.0	2.9	0.0	5.4
Produce at cost	6.7	0.0	18.7	0.0
Total farms or workers	30	35	107	111

Cambridge:	Hired workers entitled to perquisites		
	Near	Middle	Far
	per cent		
Potatoes	25.7	64.1	95.3
Other produce	30.7	40.5	46.5
Firewood	13.9	61.0	24.4
Produce at cost	26.2	19.8	0.0
Protective clothing	37.1	0.0	0.0
Land, seed, fertiliser	7.4	4.6	11.6
Use of machinery	2.0	3.8	11.6
Total workers	202	131	86

Today 54 per cent of full time male hired workers on farms in England and Wales have cottages provided (Ministry of Agriculture, Fisheries and Food, 1973), the proportion in Scotland being much higher. Farm managers, foremen and stockmen, especially cowmen, are the most likely to live in tied cottages; Giles and Mills (1970) found that 91 per cent of farm managers had houses provided. Horticultural workers are less often given accommodation by their employers, yet a recent survey has shown that 80 per cent of regular workers on fruit farms lived in tied cottages (Gardner and Nicholson, 1974). It is not usual for women or youths to be tenants of farm cottages.

As Table 8.4 shows, at least half and possibly more than 60 per cent of the regular hired workers on farms in the survey lived in tied cottages. The commonest alternative was a council house but some workers lived in their own houses or with parents or rented from other landlords. Provision of tied cottages was greater on farms near each of the towns. Only the middle Cambridge area upset this pattern, with fewer workers housed than in the more distant rural parish. It is possible that the higher premiums paid on less accessible farms were intended to compensate for fewer houses being provided.

Table 8.4   Housing of workers on survey farms

	Haverhill	Stevenage	Cambridge	Total
Tied cottage	135	133	186	454
Council house	33	39	65	137
Own house	11	11	40	62
Other rented house	11	5	12	28
Lodgings	—	1	4	5
With parents	—	11	22	33
Other (eg. caravan)	1	2	6	9
Not specified	68	16	93	177
All workers	259	218	428	905

Haverhill		Stevenage		Cambridge			
Near	Far	Near	Far	City	Near	Middle	Far
tied cottages as per cent housing specified							
80.0	64.0	67.0	64.7	68.5	59.0	47.3	56.8

The more liberal provision of tied cottages on farms near towns can be interpreted in several ways. It may be an effect of the greater demand for housing in and near towns or it may reflect the higher standards of accommodation in urban areas.

8.3.1   Effects of the housing shortage

In and near towns the housing shortage may be so acute that workers are obliged to rely on their employers to provide accommodation or, if they have a choice, the cost of alternative

71

housing would make the subsidised tied cottage doubly attractive. In remoter rural areas there may be still be some choice for the farm worker, so that fewer would be obliged to live in a tied cottage against their inclination. Some would argue that the farm worker living in a tied cottage is a captive in the sense that if he leaves the job he forfeits the house and, especially near towns, alternative accommodation is difficult to rent and too costly to buy. As Newby has pointed out, the tied cottage may facilitate mobility within agriculture but it adds to the financial barriers to outward mobility. Besides constraints of the labour market are constraints of the rural housing market which increase as urbanisation inflates house prices. The proportion of workers near towns living in tied cottages may be higher because only the 'captives' remain, those not dependent on their employers for accommodation having left already.

Often it is the availability of housing rather than its low cost which attracts workers. When the survey was carried out the rent of a tied cottage was 30p per week, that of a council house in the same area of the order of £3.00 or £3.50 a week while the wages gap between agriculture and manufacturing industry stood at £10.00 a week. A worker about to marry or with a family may be obliged to take a farm job with a house provided rather than accepting a better paid job in another industry with no accommodation provided and little prospect of finding any.

Evidence from the farm survey suggested that the tied cottage near a town was more attractive to workers than a cottage in an isolated situation. Complaints about workers quitting the farm job but refusing to vacate the tied cottage were more common on farms close to Cambridge and Stevenage, where there was a serious shortage of housing to rent, than in more rural areas with a housing surplus. Only about half the workers who had occupied tied cottages on farms near these towns had moved out on leaving the farm, although they were not always required to do so. In the most isolated areas in the Fens, where there was no new industry and a low replacement rate for workers leaving farms, fewer farmers would be expected to insist on workers leaving farm cottages when they left the job. In fact, most workers leaving farms in this area moved house also. A recent survey in *Farmers Weekly* supports the suggestion that the tied cottage is more attractive to workers if located near a town and that this leads to some abuse of the system by workers (Thompson and Gasson, 1974). In a Polish study, too, some workers had chosen to work on state farms near industrial centres only for the sake of obtaining frree housing near a town (Ignar, 1971).

8.3.2 *Quality of housing*

Whether the farm worker living in a tied cottage near a town is an unhappy victim of the housing shortage or fortunate in occupying what is virtually rent free accommodation, is a subjective issue charged with emotion. Doubtless the balance of advantages and disadvantages will depend on the individuals concerned. More objectively, it can be argued that the tied cottage near a town will be more attractive in general because it will be provided with better services and amenities.

Studying the effects of new town growth on the countryside, the Agricultural Land Service study team concluded that the condition of tied cottages in the Stevenage area had had a marked effect on the ability of farms to retain their workers in the face of increasing competition from the New Town. Local farmers and agricultural officers were all agreed that availability of tied cottages and their low rents had done much to counteract the strong attraction of high wages. Modernisation of farm cottages in particular had helped to check the serious drain on labour which had been experienced when the building of the New Town began. A parallel study of Harlow New Town at the same time showed that where workers had been lost from farms it was invariably from the least accessible holdings or those with inadequate cottages. Labour problems on farms near Harlow were slight compared with other new towns and this was attributed to the superior condition of farm cottages in the vicinity (Agricultural Land Service, 1953).

73

'In so far as low rents in rural areas are due to poorer housing conditions, they are not likely to keep workers from moving to other occupations' (Murray, 1939). While the condition of tied cottages will certainly vary a great deal from one farm to another, houses near towns will be more likely than those in isolated rural areas to have been modernised and to have all main services. Housing standards in rural areas are generally inferior to urban areas and housing in rural areas of East Anglia is considerably below the national standard for rural housing. The proportion of rural houses in the region without a hot water tap, fixed bath or water closet was double that for all rural houses in England and Wales, and in the Fens housing conditions were significantly worse with fewer than two households in three having exclusive use of the three basic amenities (East Anglia Economic Planning Council, 1968, 104–105). The quality of accommodation offered to farm workers in and near towns is likely to be better than in most rural areas and this could contribute to the greater stability of the labour force on farms near towns. Where the labour force is being reduced it is likely that workers will occupy the houses better suited to their needs with more accommodation and services and in more convenient situations while the surplus of less suitable cottages is sold or demolished.

The suggestion that competition for labour could result in more favourable treatment of workers remaining on farms was supported by the survey. Payment of premiums was more widespread on farms near the towns than in more rural areas and, in the case of Stevenage, provision of perquisites was also more liberal. Evidence from the Cambridge survey suggested that the style of labour management might be affected in more fundamental ways by the degree of urban influence. Greater provision of housing for workers on farms near the towns might be regarded as further evidence of more generous treatment of workers where competition for labour was stronger or it might be seen as the effect of an urban housing shortage on a low paid social group. The tied cottage in an urban setting may be a more attractive proposition by virtue of the provision of main services and access to town facilities. The next chapter develops this theme, considering other benefits farm workers may derive from having access to a town.

9. Accessibility to towns

Proximity to towns may itself have a significant influence on farm workers' decisions to move. Results of the survey strongly support the suggestion that access to towns is regarded favourably by farm workers and their families. It may help to hold them on farms where workers in more isolated areas would be inclined to move and perhaps leave agriculture.

9 1 Problems of rural isolation

Advantages of living near a town include access to a wider range of professional, commercial and entertainment facilities, better public transport and links with the national transport networks. Children living near urban areas are likely to have shorter journeys to school while opportunities for further education and vocational training, short of university level, which are normally available in towns, may be non-existent or only obtained with great difficulty in rural areas (Hale, 1971). Nowadays most of the drawbacks of rural living can be overcome by those with sufficient means. Heads of two-car households can drive long distances to work while wives can visit towns for shopping and other needs and transport children to extra-school activities. Unfortunately those who most need to be able to visit towns may be the least mobile. In East Anglia the elderly, unemployed and lower paid tend to be concentrated in the remoter rural areas while employment opportunities for the unskilled, cut-price shops and headquarters of the social and welfare services are mainly located in the larger towns. Although car ownership in the region is above the national average there is still a sizeable minority of households without their own means of transport and many of these will be farm workers' families.

In the Stevenage area, 15 per cent of workers leaving farms near the town and 23 per cent from less accessible areas had left for 'personal and family' reasons. Often the move had been precipitated by the wife's refusal to continue living in an isolated farm cottage without near neighbours, perhaps tied with small children and lacking any means of public or private transport. One manager of a large farm in the outer Stevenage area refused to employ prospective workers unless the wife could drive and had the use of a car since high turnover of workers in isolated cottages had proved so disruptive of the farm organisation.

Farms in the outer Stevenage area, within a few miles of other towns like Luton or Welwyn Garden City can scarcely be described as isolated in any absolute sense, yet families living there might be *effectively* isolated and this could influence their decisions to move. Other factors also contributed to the high rate of mobility due to family and personal reasons in this area. The farm workers here were younger than in the other areas so that more of the wives would be at home looking after young children. Possibly, too, the younger generation aspires to a style of life more like that of urban workers and so suffers more relative deprivation than older farm workers with rural reference groups. It was commented, too, that many of the Stevenage workers had no roots in the area and tended to move from farm to farm, not because they were particularly dissatisfied but because there was no reason for them to remain in one place rather than another. Workers with a long association with a locality and with family ties there are generally reluctant to move but once these connections are broken they may be less likely to settle anywhere.

Discussion with farmers in the Cambridge area illustrated the ways in which housing and access to the city affected labour mobility. Farmers in and near Cambridge itself were mostly of the opinion that it would be virtually impossible to engage a new worker unless a house were offered. Those who had recently advertised for labour and offered accommodation had been embarrassed by the flood of replies. The majority of workers would regard a job near Cambridge with favour since it

77

would combine a rural environment with many advantages of urban living. Farmers agreed it was not easy to find a *good* worker and commented on the difficulty of distinguishing genuine applicants from those mainly interested in the offer of a house.

Farmers in the middle area generally agreed that there were few first class workers looking for jobs but felt that the housing issue was not critical. New housing development in the area had eased the housing shortage to some extent. Besides this the increase in population had resulted in improvements in the range and quality of services available and had perhaps increased the attraction of the village for farm workers and their families. Some farmers felt that the offer of a tied cottage might help to attract and retain a good worker but the house would have to be of good quality, that is modern or modernised, well built and preferably in the main village, close to the school and shops and on the bus route. Old unmodernised cottages in outlying hamlets or in the Fen could no longer be considered an asset.

In the more remote Fen parish, farmers believed it would be difficult to find a good worker but few thought the offer of a house would attract more applicants. Here, with agricultural employment declining and population decreasing, the village seemed to be losing its attractiveness for farm workers. Younger workers preferred to live in the nearest small towns and the additional costs of rent and travel to work were presumably more than offset for them by the advantages of living in a town, where the wives would feel less isolated and might find work and children would be near a school. Older workers in this area were more content to remain in tied cottages and it is likely that they were occupying the better houses in the main village. With only one worker in three being replaced and with younger workers preferring to live elsewhere, many cottages in this parish had become empty. Some were derelict at the time of the survey and many had already been demolished in the droves. Out migration may be a cumulative process in that the more families leave, the greater the loneliness for those remaining and the stronger the economic, social and psychological pressures on them to move also.

9.2   Employment of members of farm workers' families

Perhaps the greatest advantage of good access to a town is the wider choice of employment open to members of the worker's family. In an isolated area wives may be unable to take part time jobs to supplement the family income and sons and daughters leaving school may have to choose between taking a low paid local job and leaving home.

Farmers in the Haverhill survey were able to supply information on occupations of some members of their workers' households. As Table 9.1 shows, very few were employed in agriculture. Only 8 out of 58 sons living at home worked on farms but 22 were employed in factories and others in garages, shops and building firms. Daughters in particular were attracted to the factories and some worked in shops or offices. Without the town expansion scheme, few of these young people could have found such well paid jobs locally. About half the farm workers' fathers and brothers living in the same households were employed in factories or in other town jobs, half on the land. Only two wives of workers were employed in factories but

Table 9.1 Occupations of members of Haverhill farm workers' families

	Sons	Daughters	Fathers, brothers	Wives, sisters	Total
Farm	8	–	7	11	26
Factory	22	10	6	2	40
Building	6	–	1	–	7
Garage	6	–	–	–	6
Shop	5	2	–	2	9
Office	–	3	–	1	4
Domestic	1	–	–	22	23
Other	10	1	2	3	16
All members	58	16	16	41	131

a number had part time domestic jobs or worked on the land occasionally. Most wives of farm workers, lacking their own transport and with insufficient time to make a long journey to work, were employed locally and often worked on the same farm as their husbands. Sons and daughters, being more mobile and needing full time work, were more likely to travel to work in Haverhill.

Expansion of Haverhill had had less direct influence on the lives of farmers and their families. Nearly all members of farmers' households with gainful occupations were farming in partnership or employed on the family farm. Two wives also farmed in their own right and daughters often had careers related to agriculture. Only one farmer's daughter worked in a Haverhill factory. Comparing the two groups, 78 per cent of members of farmers' households, excluding heads, were farming compared with 20 per cent of members' of farm workers' households. This emphasizes the importance of alternative employment for other members of the farm worker's family, especially the younger generation.

Bracey considered the main effect of rural industrialisation might be to reduce the entry of young people to agriculture but found little indication that farm production had suffered as a result (Bracey, 1963). Yet Carter and Hirsch found that the supply of boys in agriculture was only adequate in those areas where there was recruitment from non-rural sources, coinciding approximately with areas of greatest urban and industrial concentration. Proximity to the labour supply of towns might increase the number of youths available for agriculture but alternatively it might be suggested that farms near towns and industry provided more attractive conditions of work than areas beyond urban influence (Carter and Hirsch, 1952).

To summarise, there are a number of reasons why workers should prefer to remain on farms accessible to towns. Farmers may offer them greater incentives to dissuade them from moving to urban employment. Members of their families may find work in the town and all may benefit from access to urban services and amenities. Tied cottages located in or near towns may be more convenient and attractive than houses in isolated surroundings with no easy access to towns.

10. Conclusions

The study set out to investigate some aspects of the influence of alternative employment opportunities on the hired farm labour force. The main questions covered were the impact of growth in employment on the local farm labour supply, the ways in which occupational mobility comes about and the effects of urban influence on workers remaining on farms.

There can be little doubt that urban and industrial development in rural areas benefits the lives of farm workers through stimulating improvements in rural standards of living. Evidence from this and other studies suggests that farm workers place a positive value on access to towns. Few among them seem prepared to turn their backs on an urban civilisation. If farm workers stand to gain from urbanisation, farmers may benefit through having a more contented labour force. Until now it has been customary for farmers in industrial areas to pay premiums to keep workers from going to work in the towns. In future it may be necessary for farmers in more rural areas to offer some inducement to compensate for the disadvantages of rural living. If the tied cottage in an isolated situation is no longer acceptable to the majority of young farm workers and their wives, farmers may be obliged to find alternatives, such as paying the rent of a council house in the village or subsidising workers' transport. These practices had already been introduced on some farms in the survey.

Provision of alternative employment in rural areas must also be advantageous for the farm labour force. The main objective of any policy concerned with mobility of agricultural workers should not be to encourage or discourage occupational transfers but to improve the conditions under which such changes occur. The guiding principle, as far as the welfare of the workers is concerned, should be to increase the opportunities for choice and to reduce the constraints which are felt most severely by the under privileged. Increasing alternative employment in rural areas can help in several ways, by allowing those who are dissatisfied with farm work or who only entered agriculture because nothing else was available, to move to more congenial employment. Indirectly the growth of alternative employment may stimulate improvements in levels of earnings and conditions of employment in the traditional rural occupations and may make available facilities for vocational training. Sons and daughters of farm workers may benefit from the opportunities for training and may be able to find well paid jobs. There is still a danger that these advantages may not be shared by the most needy rural families. J. Curry warned, from experience with the Shannon industrial development scheme, that provision of alternative employment cannot be regarded as the only solution for problem rural areas since its effects are selective within the rural population (Curry, 1972). It was concluded from the Small Towns Study that the degree to which the rural population in East Anglia could benefit from industrial development would depend on their ability to commute (East Anglia Consultative Committee, 1972) or as Hathaway and Perkins remarked, the mobility process works least well for those who need it most.

As the potentially more mobile workers leave agriculture, farmers make greater efforts to attract their replacements and persuade the remaining workers to stay. Employees will find themselves in a stronger bargaining position and will receive more favourable treatment. This could result in their moving between farms in search of the best conditions. As Jones found in the north Wales study, some farm workers moved to construction sites but many who had previously been employed on poorer farms took the opportunity to move to larger and better farms in their place. Better terms of employment coupled with advantages of easy access to towns may set up currents of migration within the farm labour force. A study of Nottinghamshire farms showed that workers near the city were being attracted into Nottingham industries and their places taken by workers from farms in more agricultural areas of the

83

county, who were replaced in their turn by farm workers from Lincolnshire where there was little alternative to farm employment (Thorns, 1967). A similar migration stream was discovered from Norfolk and Suffolk to Hertfordshire farms. In the long run the labour problem for farmers located near towns or industry may be one of turnover while farmers less accessible to towns may experience greater difficulties through an absolute shortage of workers.

From the farmer's point of view, development of alternative employment in the locality must seem less welcome, although there is little firm evidence that industrial employment threatens farm output. Town expansion initially draws some workers away from farms into factories or to jobs in construction, transport or the service industries. In the present survey this effect was fairly limited in both time and space. Such developments can be detrimental to farming in the short run, hindering normal farm operations and disrupting the equilibrium of a well established farming system by a rapid turnover of workers. During this phase farmers may be obliged to make adjustments which are ultimately beneficial. Growth of alternative employment may absorb surplus labour and obviate the need for farmers to declare workers redundant. If forced to raise wages, they will dispense with the less adequate workers and so will be left with a smaller labour force of more efficient and committed workers. The fact that these changes are made sooner rather than later may give the farmers a competitive advantage over those in more rural areas where labour shortages occur later.

Perhaps the most crucial question for the agricultural industry is the selectivity of migration. The degree to which the more able and enterprising workers are differentially attracted away from farms cannot be assessed from the evidence of the survey. If the better workers are leaving the effect on agricultural productivity will, of course, be undesirable. If these workers are able to continue living in rural areas, however, the loss to rural community life may be less serious than if they were forced to migrate to distant cities.

The majority of the Scott Committee felt that one of the more harmful effects of rural industrialisation would be the attraction of young workers away from agriculture. Bracey's conclusion that new industry will affect recruitment of young workers to agriculture more than it will reduce the existing labour force was strongly supported in this study. Only one farm worker's son in seven was employed on a farm, in the Haverhill survey. Possibly town expansion causes severe initial problems for farming, receding in importance until the present generation of farm workers reaches retiring age, when it may emerge again as a more serious challenge to agriculture. Since nearly half the farm workers in the eastern region are due to retire within the next twenty years, severe labour shortages may emerge rather sooner here than in other parts of Britain.

APPENDIX

Table A1.1   Growth of employment in Haverhill, Stevenage and Cambridge 1960 to 1971

	Working population			Proportion unemployed		
	Haverhill	Stevenage	Cambridge	Haverhill	Stevenage	Cambridge
	000s			per cent		
1960	5.7	20.6	60.4	1.1	0.2	0.4
1961	6.0	22.4	60.8	0.7	0.1	0.4
1962	6.2	24.9	63.5	1.0	0.2	0.5
1963	6.6	24.7	64.2	1.1	0.5	0.8
1964	6.7	27.3	66.9	0.7	0.1	0.4
1965	7.0	27.1	67.5	0.9	0.1	0.4
1966	7.3	29.5	67.0	1.3	0.3	0.5
1967	7.3	28.8	70.7	2.1	0.8	0.7
1968	7.3	28.7	68.7	1.9	1.1	0.8
1969	7.7	31.7	76.7	1.8	0.9	0.9
1970	7.4	31.4	68.2	1.6	1.0	1.0
1971	7.9	n.a.	69.4	2.5	n.a.	2.2

Source: Department of Employment

Table A2.1   Composition of the hired farm labour force in England and Wales and the eastern region, 1969

	England and Wales	Eastern region
	per cent	per cent
Full time	70.6	70.0
Part time	12.0	11.5
Seasonal and casual	17.4	18.5
Adult males	70.0	70.9
Youths	10.6	6.4
Women and girls	19.4	22.7
All hired workers	100.0	100.0
Numbers	353 565	83 096

Source: Ministry of Agriculture, Fisheries and Food, June census 1969

Table A2.2   Composition of the hired farm labour force in survey parishes in 1969 and distance from towns.

	Haverhill		Stevenage		Cambridge			Cambridge sub-region	
	Near	Far	Near	Far	Near	Middle	Far	Accessible	Remote
				per cent of hired workers					
Full time	75.6	78.1	75.4	82.8	73.5	57.7	57.1	69.5	73.5
Part time	14.2	12.5	13.7	8.8	12.6	10.6	14.7	11.1	10.4
Seasonal	10.2	9.4	10.9	8.4	13.9	31.7	28.2	19.4	16.1
Adult males	80.0	81.7	78.2	81.4	80.8	71.3	73.4	72.5	77.2
Youths	6.8	5.3	7.6	10.2	6.6	5.1	4.5	6.1	6.4
Females	13.2	13.0	14.2	8.4	12.6	23.6	22.1	21.4	16.4
All workers	100.0	100.0	100.0	100.0	100.0	100.0	100.0	100.0	100.0
Numbers	586	936	183	215	317	237	245	6359	5248

Source: Ministry of Agriculture, Fisheries and Food, June census 1969.

Table A2.3   Age distribution of full time male hired workers in survey parishes in 1969 and distance from towns.

	Haverhill		Stevenage		Cambridge			Cambridge sub-region	
	Near	Far	Near	Far	Near	Middle	Far	Accessible	Remote
				per cent of male full time hired workers					
Under 20	7.6	5.5	9.8	11.6	7.1	7.5	7.3	7.9	7.5
20−24	6.7	8.2	5.3	10.8	10.7	9.0	12.4	9.0	9.4
25−34	16.8	16.9	23.5	21.5	10.7	19.6	21.9	15.8	18.4
35−44	22.1	19.7	21.2	26.4	22.8	26.3	24.8	22.4	22.5
45−64	42.8	45.5	36.4	26.4	46.5	36.9	30.7	41.5	38.3
65 and over	4.0	4.2	3.8	3.3	2.2	0.7	2.9	3.4	3.9
All workers	100.0	100.0	100.0	100.0	100.0	100.0	100.0	100.0	100.0
Numbers	430	709	132	121	224	133	137	4094	3690

Source: Ministry of Agriculture, Fisheries and Food, June census 1969.

Table A2.4 Changes in hired labour on farms in England and Wales and in the eastern region 1960 to 1969.

	England and Wales			Eastern region		
	1960	1969	Change	1960	1969	Change
	000s	000s	per cent	000s	000s	per cent
Regular full time						
males	317.2	200.4	−36.8	79.5	49.3	−38.0
youths	60.4	30.6	−49.5	9.8	4.5	−53.5
females	28.1	18.8	−33.1	5.7	4.3	−25.1
Regular part time						
males	38.4	21.9	−42.5	7.2	4.5	−37.8
youths	5.1	2.2	−56.9	0.7	0.2	−66.7
females	28.9	18.1	−37.4	7.5	4.8	−36.2
Seasonal, casual						
males	42.4	25.1	−64.4	9.0	5.2	−42.5
youths	4.7	4.8	+ 2.1	0.7	0.5	−26.8
females	36.8	31.6	−14.1	11.3	9.7	−13.7
Full time	405.7	249.8	−38.5	95.0	58.1	−38.9
Part time	72.4	42.2	−41.7	15.4	9.5	−38.3
Seasonal, casual	84.0	61.5	−26.8	21.0	15.4	−26.4
Adult males	398.0	247.4	−37.8	95.7	59.0	−38.4
Youths	70.2	37.7	−46.4	11.2	5.3	−52.7
Females	93.8	68.5	−27.0	24.5	18.8	−23.3
*All hired workers	562.1	353.6	−37.1	131.5	83.1	−36.7

Source: Ministry of Agriculture, Fisheries and Food, June census 1960 and 1969.

*Components do not always add up to totals due to rounding.

Table A3.1   Losses of hired farm workers in the Cambridge sub-region 1961 to 1969 and distance from towns.

Town	Accessible	Remote	Total	Numbers lost
		percentage loss		
Cambridge	30.8	39.0	35.2	2229
Huntingdon	32.0	41.5	38.7	921
Biggleswade/St. Neots	14.5	32.7	20.7	610
Ely	31.5	45.2	35.0	993
Royston/Saffron Walden	18.4	22.0	20.0	114
Newmarket	27.0	9.5	17.3	118
Haverhill	40.9	35.9	37.7	533
Total sub-region	27.3	37.5	32.5	5518

Source: Ministry of Agriculture, Fisheries and Food, June census 1961 and 1969.

Table A4.1   Losses of hired workers from survey parishes 1960/61 to 1969 and distance from towns.

	Haverhill		Stevenage		Cambridge			Cambridge sub-region	
	Near	Far	Near	Far	Near	Middle	Far	Accessible	Remote
	percentage loss of workers 1960 to 1969							1961–1969	
Full time	46.3	37.5	45.5	44.0	14.7	35.4	41.8	29.0	35.7
Part time	17.0	19.9	+13.6	36.7	33.3	62.7	36.8	27.4	34.9
Seasonal	52.0	45.0	35.5	+20.0	32.3	29.8	11.5	20.8	45.1
Adult men	44.6	35.2	37.6	42.8	18.0	32.5	30.0	31.0	35.5
Youths	60.5	59.0	54.9	45.4	25.0	63.6	70.3	32.0	49.7
Females	24.5	30.3	43.5	11.1	31.0	45.6	34.1	3.2	39.4
All hired workers	44.2	36.7	40.2	42.0	20.4	38.6	34.8	27.3	37.5
Numbers lost	463	541	123	148	81	149	131	2401	3117

Source: Ministry of Agriculture, Fisheries and Food, June census 1960, 1961 and 1969.

Table A4.2   Length of service of employees on survey farms and distance from towns.

Years employed on same farm	Haverhill Near	Haverhill Far	Stevenage Near	Stevenage Far	Cambridge Near	Cambridge Middle	Cambridge Far	England and Wales 1972
			per cent	of hired	workers			
Under 2	15.0	2.4	22.7	21.8	7.8	9.1	12.8	15.4
2	4.6	1.6	9.3	7.3	12.9	6.8	4.6	7.6
3–4	5.7	14.4	14.4	10.0	12.1	14.4	3.5	11.5
5–9	18.4	15.2	9.3	20.0	25.8	15.9	16.3	18.1
10–14	10.4	16.0	10.3	10.0	11.2	9.9	16.3	13.9
15–19	9.2	12.0	8.2	8.2	12.9	9.1	19.8	8.6
20 and over	36.7	38.4	25.8	22.7	17.3	34.8	26.7	21.7
Not known	–	–	–	–	–	–	–	3.2
All workers	100.0	100.0	100.0	100.0	100.0	100.0	100.0	100.0
Numbers	87	125	97	110	116	132	86	n.a.

Source: (England and Wales) Ministry of Agriculture, Fisheries and Food, 1973, *Agricultural Labour in England and Wales: Earnings, Hours and Numbers of Persons*

Table A5.1   Losses of seasonal labour in the Cambridge sub-region 1961 to 1969 and distance from towns.

	Accessible	Remote	Total
	percentage loss		
Adult men	37.7	46.5	41.7
Youths	15.9	36.4	28.2
Females	3.3	44.7	25.2
Cambridge	30.0	53.0	43.5
Huntingdon	45.1	49.0	47.9
Biggleswade/St. Neots	+	27.3	3.6
Ely	23.9	33.0	26.5
Royston/Saffron Walden	26.3	48.2	35.4
Newmarket	+	29.7	2.8
Haverhill	40.0	25.8	31.2
Sub-region	20.8	45.1	32.9

Source: Ministry of Agriculture, Fisheries and Food, June census 1961 and 1969.

+ = small gain

90

REFERENCES

AGRICULTURAL DEVELOPMENT AND ADVISORY SERVICE, 1973, *Agriculture in the Urban Fringe*, Ministry of Agriculture, Fisheries and Food

AGRICULTURAL LAND SERVICE, 1951, *The Effects of Town Growth on the Countryside: Study No. 1—Scunthorpe, Lincolnshire*, Ministry of Agriculture and Fisheries

AGRICULTURAL LAND SERVICE, 1953, *The Effects of Town Growth on the Countryside: Study No. 2—The New Towns of Stevenage, Harlow and Crawley*, Ministry of Agriculture and Fisheries

AGRICULTURE EDC, 1972, *Agricultural Manpower in England and Wales*, National Economic Development Office, HMSO

BELLERBY, J.R., 1956, *Agriculture and Industry Relative Income*, Macmillan

BELLERBY, J.R., 1958, 'The distribution of manpower in agriculture and industry 1851—1951', *Farm Economist*, 9(1): 1—11

BESSELL, J.E., 1972, *The Younger Worker in Agriculture: Projections to 1980*, National Economic Development Office, HMSO

BISHOP, C.E., (ed.) 1965, *Geographic and Occupational Mobility of Rural Manpower*, OECD Documentation in Agriculture and Food No. 75, Paris

BLACK, M., 1968, 'Agricultural labour in an expanding economy', *Journal of Agricultural Economics*, 19(1):59—76

BRACEY, H.E., 1963, *Industry in the Countryside*, Faber and Faber for the Acton Society Trust; see also

BRACEY, H.E., 1970, *People and the Countryside*, Routledge and Kegan Paul

BRITTON, D.K. and SMITH, J.H., 1947, 'Farm labour: Problems of age composition and recruitment', *Farm Economist*, 5(11 and 12): 204—209

BUTCHER, F., 1972, 'We pay: £1 245 a year—and a free house', *Farmers Weekly*, September 15: 58—61

CARTER, J. and HIRSCH, G.P., 1952, *Juvenile Labour in Agriculture*, Oxford University Institute for Research in Agricultural Economics

COWIE, W.J.G. and GILES, A.K., 1957, *An Inquiry into Reasons for 'The Drift from the Land'*, University of Bristol Department of Economics (Agricultural Economics) Selected Papers in Agricultural Economics 5(3)

COWLING, K., 1969, 'Agricultural labour supply and the business cycle: some regional predictions', *Symposium on Agricultural Manpower,* National Economic Development Office, HMSO, p. 10–17

CURRY, J., 1972, 'Effects of non-farm employment in rural areas', *Farm and Food Research,* January–February: 4–7

DRUDY, P.J. and WALLACE, D.B., 1972, *The Causes and Consequences of Rural Depopulation: Case Studies of Declining Communities,* Unpublished paper presented at Third World Congress of Rural Sociology, Baton Rouge, Louisiana

EAST ANGLIA CONSULTATIVE COMMITTEE and EAST ANGLIA ECONOMIC PLANNING COUNCIL, 1972, *Small Towns Study,* East Anglia Consultative Committee and East Anglia Economic Planning Council, Cambridge

EAST ANGLIA ECONOMIC PLANNING COUNCIL, 1968, *East Anglia–A Study,* Department of Economic Affairs, HMSO

EASTWOOD, T., 1951, *Industry in the Country Towns of Norfolk and Suffolk,* Oxford University Press

Farmers Weekly, 1973a, 'Oil rig pay packets lure Scots workers', March 16:52

Farmers Weekly, 1973b, 'Strawberry growers pay retainers', April 6:57

Farmers Weekly, 1973c, 'Transport and labour troubles threaten earlies', April 13:51

GARBETT-EDWARDS, D.P., 1972, 'The establishment of new industries (with particular reference to recent experience in Mid-Wales)' in J. Ashton and W.H. Long, (eds.) *The Remoter Rural Areas of Britain,* University of Newcastle-upon-Tyne, p. 50–73

GARDNER, F.N., and NICHOLSON, J.A.H., 1974, Report on manpower and labour management in the United Kingdom fruit industry, Wye College School of Rural Economics and Related Studies, to be published

GASSON, R.M., 1966, *The Influence of Urbanisation on Farm Ownership and Practice,* Wye College Studies in Rural Land Use No. 7

GASSON, R.M., 1968, 'Occupations chosen by the sons of farmers', *Journal of Agricultural Economics,* 19(3): 317–326

GASSON, R.M., 1969a, 'The choice of farming as an occupation', *Sociologia Ruralis,* 9(2): 146–166

GASSON, R.M., 1969b, *Occupational Immobility of Small Farmers*, Cambridge University Department of Land Economy, Farm Economics Branch

GASSON, R.M., 1973, 'Goals and values of farmers', *Journal of Agricultural Economics*, 24(3): 521–537

GILES, A.K. and COWIE, W.J.G., 1961, 'Some social and economic aspects of agricultural workers' accommodation', *Journal of Agricultural Economics*, 14(2): 147–169; and see also
COWIE, W.J.G. and GILES, A.K., 1960, *Accommodation of Agricultural Workers*, University of Bristol Department of Economics (Agricultural Economics)

GILES, A.K. and MILLS, F.D., 1970, *Farm Managers: Part I*, University of Reading Department of Agricultural Economics, Miscellaneous Study No. 47

GREEN, R.J. and AYTON, J.B., 1967, *Changes in the Pattern of Rural Settlements*, Research Conference on Planning for the Changing Countryside, Town Planning Institute

HALL, W.R., 1970, *Agriculture and the Farming Community in an Urban-Rural Fringe Area*, Unpublished dissertation, University of Reading Agricultural Extension Centre

HALE, S., 1971, *The Idle Hill: A Prospect for Young Workers in a Rural Area*, Herefordshire Community Council, Bedford Square Press

HATHAWAY, D.E. and PERKINS, B.B., 1968 'Occupational mobility and migration from agriculture', in *Rural Poverty in the United States*, Report by the President's Advisory Commission on Rural Poverty, Washington DC, p 185–237

HAWKESWORTH, R.I., 1971, *A Study of the Mobility of Farm Labour in South-East Nottinghamshire 1965–1970*, Unpublished M.Sc. thesis, University of Nottingham Department of Agricultural Economics

HEATH, C.E. and WHITBY, M.C., 1969, *The Changing Agricultural Labour Force: Implications for Training*, University of Newcastle-upon-Tyne, Agricultural Adjustment Bulletin No. 10

HIRSCH, G.P., 1951, 'Migration from the land in England and Wales', *Farm Economist*, 6(9): 270–280

HIRSCH, G.P., 1955, 'Labour on the land in England and Wales', *Farm Economist*, 8(2): 13–24

MOBILITY OF FARM WORKERS

HODSDON, D., 1969, 'Manpower in agriculture' in *A Discussion of Current Policies and the Future Structure of Agriculture*, University of Newcastle-upon-Tyne, Agricultural Adjustment Unit Bulletin No. 8, p. 55–68

HUGHES, J.D., 1957, 'A note on the decline in numbers of farmworkers in Great Britain', *Farm Economist*, 8(9): 34–39

IGNAR, M., 1971, 'Changes in the situation of workers employed on State farms in regions under industrialisation', *Symposium for Research on Regions under Industrialisation*, Polish Academy of Sciences, Warsaw, p. 265–272

INTERNATIONAL LABOUR OFFICE, 1960, *Why Labour Leaves the Land*, I.L.O. Studies and Reports New Series No. 59, Geneva

JONES, W.D., 1972, 'The impact of public works schemes on farming: a case study relating to a reservoir and a power station in North Wales', *Journal of Agricultural Economics*, 23(1): 1–13

KRIER, H., 1961, *Rural Manpower and Industrial Development: Adaptation and Training*, OEEC

KOTTER, H., 1962, 'Economic and social implications of rural industrialisation', *International Labour Review*, 86 (July–December): 1–14

LUCEY, D.I. and KALDOR, D.R., 1969, *Rural Industrialisation—The Impact of Industrialisation on Two Rural Communities in Western Ireland*, Geoffrey Chapman

McINTOSH, F., 1972, 'A survey of workers leaving Scottish farms', *Scottish Agricultural Economics*, 22: 147–152

MINISTRY OF AGRICULTURE,FISHERIES AND FOOD, 1967, *The Changing Structure of the Agricultural Labour Force in England and Wales*, HMSO

MINISTRY OF AGRICULTURE, FISHERIES AND FOOD, 1968, *The Availability of Labour in Agriculture*, Memorandum to the Select Committee on Agriculture, 10 April 1968, House of Commons Session 1967/8, HMSO

MINISTRY OF AGRICULTURE, FISHERIES AND FOOD, 1973, *Agricultural Labour in England and Wales: Earnings, Hours and Numbers of Persons*, MAFF

MOSELEY, M.J., 1973, 'The impact of growth centres in rural regions: II—An analysis of spatial "flows" in East Anglia', *Regional Studies*, 7(1): 77–94

MURRAY, K.A.H., 1939, *The Economics of the Labour Problem*, Fourth Oxford Farming Conference, University of Oxford, p. 1–11

NALSON, J.S., 1968, *Mobility of Farm Families. A Study of Occupational and Residential Mobility in an Upland Area of England*, Manchester University Press

NARDECCHIA, T.J., 1969, *Evidence of the Nuthampstead Preservation Society*, Commission on the Third London Airport, Papers and Proceedings 4, Stage II Local Hearings: Nuthampstead, HMSO

NEWBY, H., 1972a, 'The low earnings of agricultural workers: a sociological approach', *Journal of Agricultural Economics*, 23(1): 15—24

NEWBY, H., 1972b, 'Agricultural workers in the class structure', *The Sociological Review*, 20(3) (New Series): 413—439

ORWIN, C.S., 1938, 'The demands for labour in agriculture', *The Scottish Journal of Agriculture*, 21(4): 1—5

PEDLEY, W.H., 1942, *Labour on the Land: A Study of the Developments Between the Two Great Wars*, P.S. King and Staples Ltd.

PICKARD, D., 1972, 'Attitudes to training in agriculture', *Journal of Agricultural Labour Science 1(1): 15—23

POWER, A.P. and HARRIS, S.A., 1973, *Agricultural Expansion in the United Kingdom with Declining Manual Labour Resources*, HMSO

PRIEBE, H., 1969, 'The modern family farm and its problems: with particular reference to the Federal German Republic' in U. Papi and C. Nunn (eds.) *Economic Problems of Agriculture in Industrial Societies*, Proceedings of Conference of International Economic Association, Macmillan, Chapter 12

READING UNIVERSITY DEPARTMENT OF AGRICULTURAL ECONOMICS AND MANAGEMENT, 1971, *Milton Keynes Revisited: 1971*, University of Reading Department of Agricultural Economics and Management, Miscellaneous Study No. 51

REPORT OF THE COMMITTEE ON LAND UTILISATION IN RURAL AREAS (SCOTT REPORT), 1942, Cmd. 6378, HMSO

SAVILLE, J., 1957, *Rural Depopulation in England and Wales 1851—1951*, Dartington Hall Studies in Rural Sociology, Routledge and Kegan Paul

TAYLOR, R.C., 1969, 'Migration and motivation: a study of determinants and types' in J.A. Jackson (ed.) *Migration*, Cambridge University Press, Chapter 5

THOMAS, W.J., 1965, 'The changing structure of agriculture's labour force', *Proceedings of the International Conference of Agricultural Economists*, 12: 298—330

MOBILITY OF FARM WORKERS

THOMPSON, M.C. and GASSON, R.M., 1974, 'Do we really need the tied cottage?'. *Farmers Weekly*, January 25: v—xxi.

THORNS, D.C., 1967, *Social Stratification and Social Mobility in a Rural Area*, Unpublished M.A. thesis, University of Exeter

TURNER, D.M., 1966, *The Inter-relationships of Urban and Rural Communities*, Unpublished Ph.D. thesis, Cambridge University Department of Land Economy

WAGSTAFF, H.R., 1971, 'Recruitment and losses of farm workers', *Scottish Agricultural Economics*, 21: 7—16

WALLACE, D.B. and DRUDY, P.J., 1972, *Social Problems of Rural Communities*, Agricultural Adjustment Unit Conference Paper 10, University of Newcastle-upon-Tyne

WALSH, B.M., 1971, 'Economic and demographic adjustment of the Irish agricultural labour force, 1961—1966,' *Irish Journal of Agricultural Economics and Rural Sociology*, 3(2): 113—124

WEST SUFFOLK COUNTY PLANNING DEPARTMENT, 1968, *People in Haverhill. A Report on the Population in 1966*, West Suffolk County Council, Bury St Edmunds

WHETHAM, E., 1960, *The Economic Background to Agricultural Policy*, Cambridge University Press

WHITBY, M.C., 1966, 'Farmers in England and Wales 1921—1961. Changes in number and age composition', *Farm Economist*, 11(2): 83—94

WHITBY, M.C., 1967, 'Labour mobility and training in agriculture', *Westminster Bank Review*, August: 43—51

WOODS, K.S., 1968, *Development of Country Towns in the South-west Midlands during the 1960s*, University of Oxford Agricultural Economics Research Institute